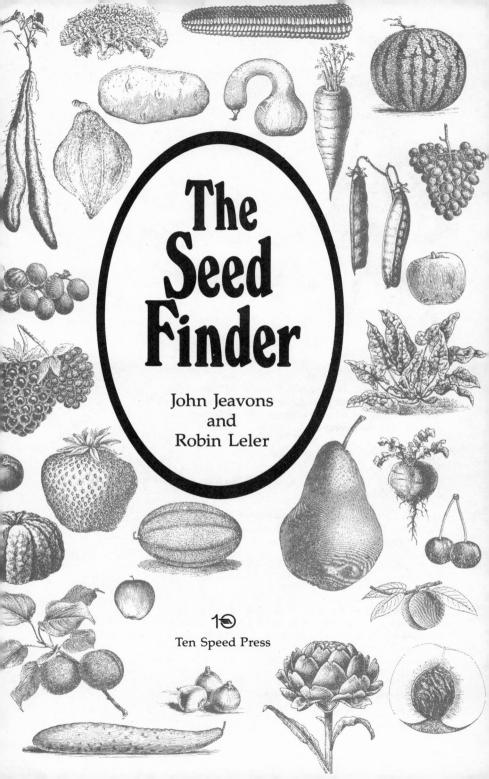

The Seed Finder

John Jeavons
and
Robin Leler

Ten Speed Press

Long Lemon Carrot
(1/5 size)

1⊜
TEN SPEED PRESS
P.O. Box 7123
Berkeley, California 94707

You may order single copies prepaid direct from the publisher
for $4.95 + $.75 per copy for postage and handling (California
residents add 6% state sales tax; Bay Area residents add 6½%).

Library of Congress Catalog Number: 83-40026
ISBN: 0-89815-100-7

Beverly Anderson Graphic Design
Type set by Joanne Shwed at Green Mountain Graphics
Engravings are from THE VEGETABLE GARDEN and are used with the
permission of The Jeavons-Leler Press, 5798 Ridgewood Rd., Willits, CA 95490.
Additional drawings by Pedro J. Gonzalez (p. 46), and from the HANDBOOK
OF PLANT AND FLORAL ORNAMENT, Dover Publications, Inc. (pp. 112
and 134).

Printed in the United States of America
10   9   8   7   6   5   4   3   3   2   1

CONTENTS

Seed Companies

Introduction *vi*
Abundant Life   3
Burpee   11
Early   23
Epicure   29
Exotica   30
Henry Field   31
Gurney   43
Johnny's Selected Seeds   55
Meadowbrook Herbs   61
Nourse Farms   62
Park's   63
Redwood City   80
Seed Savers Exchange   88
Shumway   89
Stark Brothers   101
Stokes   108
Sutton's   113
Vermont Bean   126
Tree Crops   131
Wilson Brothers   135
Dave Wilson   136

Tool Catalogs   142

Smith and Hawken
Walt Nicke

Bibliography   143
Abbreviated Index   146

Tips From The Top Of The World

Asparagus   4
Snap Beans   8
Lima Beans   10
Beets   14
Broccoli   20
Brussels Sprouts   24
Cabbage   26
Carrots   28
Cauliflower   36
Celery   40
Chard   42
Collards   46
Corn   50
Cucumbers   52
Eggplant   58
Garlic   60
Gourds   64
Lettuce   70
Melons   74
Onions   78
Parsley   84
Parsnips   86
Peanuts   90
Peas   92
Peppers, sweet   94
Peppers, hot   96
Potatoes, Irish   100
Potatoes, Sweet   104
Pumpkins   106
Radishes   110
Raspberries   112
Rhubarb   116
Spinach   118
Squash, Summer   122
Squash, Winter   128
Strawberries   130
Sunflowers   134
Tomatoes   138
Turnips and Rutabagas   141

INTRODUCTION

WE HAVE ENJOYED GROWING food gardens of all sorts for over ten years and have made it our profession to be involved with small-scale food production at every level: growing our own food, researching the biodynamic/French intensive method, and managing an educational center in Palo Alto, California that teaches garden and homestead classes and sells garden seeds by the teaspoon like penny candy. We've come to know seed varieties quite intimately and have developed the greatest respect for many underutilized varieties and for the seed companies that continue to offer them.

Several years ago we were fortunate to come across a copy of *The Vegetable Garden* (see Bibliography), a huge volume nearly one hundred years old, compiled by the Vilmorin family, founders of one of the oldest and most respected seed houses in the world. We had never seen such detailed growing directions, nor so many plant varieties. Many of the "Heritage" varieties they described then are still popular today. For example, out of more than one hundred kinds of garden peas, Laxton, Marvel and Telegraph are still grown. Even the delicious "new" Sugar Snap Pea harks back to thirty plus varieties of sugar pea listed in 1885.

We assembled *The Seed Finder* to highlight those seed companies that stock the fast disappearing home-garden varieties—those varieties best known for flavor, or tenderness, or productivity, or drought tolerance, or other qualities. "Improved" varieties that grow bigger are not necessarily better. Nor do we grow those that ship well or grow more uniformly or are tougher. We continually search out varieties that do well in our region, but may never be listed in "national" catalogs.

As this book took shape it became an increasingly useful guide for ourselves at seed ordering time when we ended up asking each other "Do you remember where you saw the shorter season sweet potato or the chrysanthemums from seed?" The consistent arrangement of

The Seed Finder makes it much easier to flip through than twenty seed catalogs.

Listings are by no means complete, but by looking for your particular interests you should get a clear idea of who emphasizes gourmet carrots or the hottest chili peppers. Of course you should order those catalogs that interest you for more detail than we provide. Our listings are highly selective. Only open-pollinated (non-hybrid) offerings are listed (see "Why Not Hybrids?" p. 145) and while many seed companies offer the same variety (such as Golden Bantam Corn or Bloomsdale Long Standing Spinach), we did not list it over and over, preferring to list what was unique to a particular company. We hope to expand on this first edition, adding a few more seed companies and updating our listings from year to year. Especially exciting varieties we have marked with a ★.

In addition to the big nationally-known seed companies, we appreciate the many small seed companies that offer special and under-utilized crops. A few are especially dedicated to finding, preserving and promoting hardy old-fashioned or "Heritage" seeds that are especially valuable in home gardens. Their prices are reasonable because packets and catalogs are not as colorful. You can expect more specialized information on wild and native type plants and the newly discovered exotics only from these smaller seedsmen and women.

Few seed companies today grow their own seeds. Our seeds come from growers around the world. Unfortunately the trend is towards dealing in large quantities of fewer types. Many valuable crops will only be kept alive if home gardeners continue to grow them, saving and sharing seeds of these strains. We've included several references on seed collection in the bibliography in the back.

With all best wishes for a bountiful garden.

John Jeavons   *Robin Leler*   January, 1983

TIPS

How We Came to the "Top Of The World"

After John spent eight and one-half years doing mini-farm research on a donated site, the garden was urbanized and turned into a parking lot. We decided to move from the city and began a two-year search for the perfect piece of land; one with good water, fair soil, a warm southern exposure and a nice community. Two years turned up a lot of dead ends, but finally a chance ad brought us to a wooded 20 acres perched near the top of a small mountain. The view was so beautiful that we did not mind much its steepness (walking from the house to the garden is 200 feet or the equivalent of 20 flights of stairs), or the rockiness of the soil. Love can be a little blind! The place is a well-known lookout for local teenagers and even has a "kissing bench" growing between two trees. They call the land "Top of the World," partly because the valley below often fills with a thick white cloud layer and the converging air currents make it a favorite soaring spot for turkey vultures and hawks.

We bought "Top of the World" and set to work growing food on the side of a mountain. One year later we are happily settled. The garden survived its first winter with 82 inches of rain and winds up to 70 miles per hour. Now 80 beds have been cleared of rocks, dug and planted with crops ordered from many of the seed houses described in this book. We gladly hike the steep hills, watch out for rattlesnakes and nurture a spring that is unfortunately at the bottom end of the property. We are still in love with the view and have even built our composting privy and solar shower towards it.

We now offer monthly tours of our new mini-farm. Through these tours and weekly classes we taught at our urban site, we have talked with hundreds of people about gardening. "Tips from the Top of the World" is our private collection of garden tidbits we have collected from our own and others' experiences. We hope they will help you to grow food wherever you find yourself.

**Each seed company's listing
is divided into the following
categories:**

Vegetables. Artichokes to Turnips in
      alphabetical order including
      "Herbs," "Greens," and "Melons."

Useful Plants. Non-food plants such
      as gourds, cotton and tobacco.

Fruits. Fruit trees, grapes and berries.

Nut Trees.

Flowers. Annuals and perennials. This
      section is a smorgasbord.

Ornamentals. Flowering shrubs, shade
      trees and hedges.

Forage, Grains and Cover Crops.

Tools, Books and Garden Aids.

Especially exciting items are marked
with a star.

Trophy Tomato

Drawings are natural size unless noted.

Abundant Life Seed Foundation
P.O. Box 772
Port Townsend, WA 98368

$2 for catalog and
informative newsletter

Abundant Life is much more than a seed company. They are actively
involved in "regionalizing" seeds in the Pacific Northwest (Oregon,
Washington, Northern California), searching out and promoting trees,
flowers, shrubs, vegetables and so-called weeds that grow easily and
naturally. You will not find many of their offerings in the local
supermarket, yet they are not exotic. Growing and using these plants
is a process of self-education.

VEGETABLES

Beans
- Dried
  - Adzuki Express Red
  - Bandy Lima—Hopi type, mixed colors
  - Cranberry Horticultural
  - Fiskeby V Soybean—small seeded, short maturing
  - Jacob's Cattle
  - Jones Blackeye Cowpea
  - Paint (Yellow Eye)—drought resistant, early maturing
  - Pinto
  - Red Cloud Kidney—early maturing
  - Speckled Bale
  - Texas Pink
  - Windsor Fava—very large seed
  - Windsor Fava—very large seed
  - Zebra Horticultural
- Snap
  - Louisiana Purple Pod
  - Oregon Giant Pole
  - Pencil Pod Black Bush—stringless yellow wax
  - Royalty Purple Pod
  - Scarlet Runner

Beets
- Lutz Greenleaf—very large, winter keeper
- Winter Keeper—grow greens in cold weather

Cabbage Family
- Cabbage
  - Chieftain Savoy
  - Mammoth Red Rock
- Cauliflower
  - English Winter
  - Veitch Autumn Giant

continued

Giant Dutch Asparagus (1/4 size)

Asparagus

Asparagus likes a fertile soil. Transplant roots on 12-inch centers with crowns of the plants 2 inches deep. Use roots when possible, since raising plants from seed takes 2-3 years. Fertilize in early spring. Harvest asparagus by cutting above the soil. The yield of a 10 square foot plot (2 feet by 5 feet) of mature plants, by the fourth year may range from 2-4 pounds.

• TIPS FROM THE TOP OF THE WORLD •

*Summer Savory
(1/8 size;
detached branch, natural size)*

Cabbage continued

Kale

Russian Red — rare
Siberian
Spring
Tall Green Curled
Thousand Headed — winter hardy

Carrots

Amsterdam Forcing — good for winter growing under greenhouse
Black Afghan — purple skin, white interior
Early Scarlet Horn — small, for greenhouse forcing
Jones Coreless
Red Elephant
Scarlet Nantes

Corn

Black Aztec — white when fresh, turns blue-green when dry
Country Gentleman
Doring
Golden Midget
Hopi Blue — an ancient strain
Improved Golden Bantam
Jones Ornamental Flint
Mandan Bride — dry, early maturing, multi-colored, for cornmeal

Cucumbers

Armenian Yard-Long
Early Russian — very early pickling variety
Lemon

Greens

Chard — Rhubarb Red
Chicory
New Zealand Spinach — tastes like spinach though it is much hardier, growing well summer and winter
Spinach

Norfolk — very hardy
Winter Bloomsdale

Vegetable Marrow
(1/8 size)

Herbs
Applemint
Caraway
Corsican Rue
Dyers Chamomile
Dyers Woodruff
Feverfew
French Lavender
Golden Yarrow
Horehound
Jacob's Ladder
Lamb's Ears—wonderful soft and floppy leaves
Lamb's Quarters—a highly nutritious weed
Lemon Balm
Marshmallow—the roots were ground up to make
    marshmallows
Miner's Lettuce—very tasty
Mugwort
Pineapple Weed
Purslane
Roman Chamomile
Safflower
Shepherds Purse
Shoo-fly Plant—said to repel white flies but also a very pretty
    flowering plant that reseeds easily
St. John's Wort
Sweet Woodruff
Valerian
Wild Indigo
Wintergreen
Winter Thyme

Pear-shaped Onion (1/3 size)

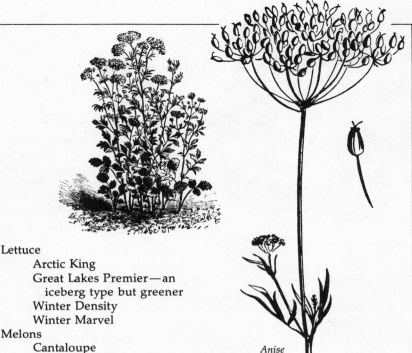

Anise
(scale not shown)

Lettuce
> Arctic King
> Great Lakes Premier—an
> > iceberg type but greener
> Winter Density
> Winter Marvel

Melons
> Cantaloupe
> > Early Hanover
> > Oregon Delicious
> Watermelon
> > Harris Earliest
> > Northern Sweet

Onions
> Early Yellow
> Egyptian Multiplier—little bulblets form atop the flower stalks
> and can be planted for onions the next season
> Oregon Yellow Danvers—long storage
> Southport Red Globe—good storage

Peas
> Alaska—very early, good dried peas
> Northern Sweet—tasty, productive, largest pod
> Sugar Snap
> Wando—heat tolerant

Peppers
> Cayenne Hot
> Sweet Chocolate Bell

Radish
> Daikon
> Winter Long Miyako—hardy long white

Rutabagas
> Laurentian—good storage

continued

Mont d'Or Dwarf Butter Bean
(1/8 size)

Snap Beans

Also called green beans though some are purple and yellow. Snap beans are an easy nutritious garden standby. Kentucky Wonders are probably the best known and do well in hot summers. Blue Lake, Tenderpod and Romano have good flavor. Bush and pole varieties have always yielded equally for us. Bush varieties save time spent trellising but pole varieties can be harvested without stooping and children are delighted by the forts they can grow with the tangling vines, especially the lovely scarlet runner beans. Bush beans are planted on 3-inch centers. Pole beans are planted 4 inches apart in beds 2 feet wide. If you put your trellis on a slant the beans will hang straight down, making them easier to see and harvest. The yield ranges from 7-11 pounds from 10 square feet.

• TIPS FROM THE TOP OF THE WORLD •

Squash
    Delicatessen—small, good flavor, good storage
    Pumpkin
        Jack O' Lantern
        Small Sugar—for pies
    Spaghetti
    Sweetmeat—excellent flavor and
      stores well
    Warted Green Hubbard—stores well
Sunflowers
    Sundak—early
Tomatoes
    Coldset
    Earliana
    Pink Cherry
    Yellow Pear
Turnips
    Chop Suey Green
    Golden Ball

French Horn, or Early
Short Horn, Carrot
(1/5 size)

OTHER USEFUL PLANTS

Broomcorn—grows like corn but tassels are dried and tied together to make a soft broom

Jojoba

FRUITS

Blue Elderberry
Himalaya Blackberry Shrub
Red Elderberry
Red-flowering Currant Shrub
Thimble Blackberry

FLOWERS

Black-eyed Susan
Bluebells
Calendula
Canterbury Bells
Fireweed
Flowering Tobacco
Giant Vetch
Job's Tears
Jupiter's Beard—fragrant red valerian, rockery plant
Lily of the Valley
Perennial Sweet Pea
    continued

*English Horn, or
Early Half-long
Scarlet, Carrot
(1/5 size)*

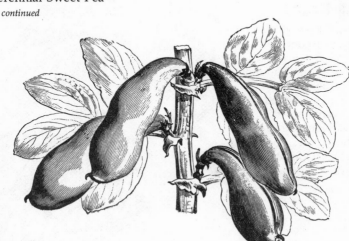

Broad Windsor Bean (1/3 size)

continued
Rock Rose—drought hardy shrub with big delicate poppy-like flowers,
  pink and yellow are quite popular
Scotch Broom
Slender Vetch
Snapdragon Mixture
Strawflower Mixture
Tiger Lily
Yellow Monkey Flower

ORNAMENTALS — TREES

Cedar
Coast Redwood

Lima Beans

Limas do best where
summers are long and hot.
Ten square feet will
produce about 2 pounds
of dried beans. Bush
varieties are planted on
6-inch centers and
pole varieties are grown
8 inches apart in beds
2-2½ feet wide. We like
the lovely "Speckled"
Limas.

Large Lima Kidney Bean
(1/12 size)

Burpee Seed Company
300 Park Ave.
Warminster, PA 18991

Burpee is among the world's largest seed companies and perhaps the best known. For our seed store in Palo Alto about half the stock is ordered from Burpee because they offer a grand selection, service is good, they handle large orders at very good prices (why not start a seed-buying club in your neighborhood?) and seeds are not generally treated with fungicides or other unnecessary chemicals. It is sometimes difficult to get a catalog from them, but once you have ordered from them you will be on their mailing list for years. The catalog is in full color and they emphasize all the popular flowers and vegetables. Offerings that do best in most all climates and soils are specially marked. Days to maturity are always noted but we've found them to be for ideal summer growing conditions.

VEGETABLES

Artichokes
    Globe
    Jerusalem—a very easy-to-grow root crop
Beans
    Dried
        Berken Mung—90 days
        Cowpeas
            California Blackeye—75 days, good yielder
            Purple Hull—78 days
            Queen Anne—68 days, early
        Dwarf Horticultural
        Garbanzo—100 days
      ★ Long Pod Bush Fava—85 days
        Pinto
      ★ Prize Bush Soybean—85 days, early
        Red Kidney
        White Kidney
        White Marrowfat
    Lima
        Baby Fordhook® Bush—70 days
        Burpee's Best Pole—92 days
        Fordhook® Large-seeded Bush—75 days
    Snap
        Burpee Golden Pole—60 days
        Burpee's Brittle Wax Yellow Bush—52 days
        Burpee's Tenderpod Bush Green—50 days
        Greensleeves Bush Green—56 days
        Rustproof Golden Wax Yellow Bush—50 days

Beets
    Burpee's Golden—55 days
    Burpee's Red Ball—60 days
    Lutz Green Leaf Winter Keeper—80 days
Cabbage Family
    Burpee's Surehead Winter Cabbage—storage variety
    Dwarf Siberian Kale—65 days
    Green Goliath Broccoli—55 days
    Pak Choi—2 varieties
    Purple Head Cauliflower—82 days
Carrots
    Burpee's Goldinhart Red Cored Chantenay—70 days
    Gold Pak—76 days, 8 to 9 inches
    Imperator—75 days, 8 to 9 inches long
    ★ Short 'n Sweet—68 days, 3½ to 4 inches, does well
        in heavy soils
Celtuce
Chicory—2 selections
Cucumbers
    Burpee Pickler—53 days
    Burpee's Sunnybrook—60 days, one of our favorites
    Bush Champion—60 days
    Lemon—65 days
Garlic
    Elephant
    Extra Select Sets
Greens
    Chard
        Fordhook® Giant Swiss
            —60 days, very good
    Endive
        Giant Fringed Oyster—90 days
    Parsley
        Extra Curled Dwarf—85 days
    Spinach
        Bloomsdale Long-standing
            —slow to bolt
        Malabar "climbing"—70 days
        Winter Bloomsdale—45 days
    Thick-leaved Dandelion—95 days
Horseradish
    Malimer Kren

Lettuce
  Burpee Bibb—75 days
  Fordhook® Butterhead—78 days
  Great Lakes Crisp-head—90 days
  Royal Oakleaf Loosehead—50 days, heat resistant, unique leaves
Melons
  Golden Beauty Casaba—120 days
  Haogen—86 days, green-flesh, smooth skin, handles raised bed
    mini-climate best of cantaloupes
  Honeydew—110 days
  New Hampshire Midget Watermelon—70 days, small,
    eating size
Mushroom Spawn
Okra
  Dwarf Green Long Pod—52 days
Onions
  Ebenezer—105 days, strong flavor
Peas
  Alaska—55 days, early
  Burpeeana Early Bush—63 days
  Maestro Bush—61 days, powdery
    mildew and disease resistant
  Oregon Sugar Edible Pod—68 days
  Sugar Snap Pole—70 days
  Wando Bush—68 days, heat and
    cold tolerant

*Small Early Yellow
Turnip Radish
(1/3 size)*

Peanuts
  Jumbo Virginia—120 days
Peppers
  Burpee's Early Pimento—65 days
  Burpee's Fordhook® Sweet Green Bell—66 days
  Golden Calwonder Sweet Bell—72 days
  Long Red Cayenne—72 days
  Sweet Cherry—78 days
Potatoes
  Kennebec
  Red Pontiac
  White Cobbler
Potatoes, sweet
  Bush Porto Rico
  Centennial
Radish
  French Breakfast
  Round Black Spanish
  White Chinese
  White Icicle   *continued*

*True Shallot
(1/2 size)*

Beets

Beets come in all shapes, sizes and colors. We particularly like Cylindra beets. They yield higher because of the elongated shape, without losing flavor or tenderness. We rarely have to peel them because so little of the top is exposed above ground. Cylindra beets yield 22- 54 pounds for roots and 11-27 pounds for tops, from 10 square feet. Plant seeds on 3- to 4-inch centers. Golden beets are a nice visual treat. They are creamy yellow inside and a golden orange outside. Both roots and tops are slightly milder tasting than red beets. For round beets expect a yield of 11-26 pounds from 10 square feet. Our favorite way to cook beets is by steaming in about ½ cup water and ½ cup orange juice.

Large Blood-red Beet
(1/5 size)

• TIPS FROM THE TOP OF THE WORLD •

continued
Squash
Burpee's Bush Table Queen Acorn—80 days
Burpee's Butterbush Butternut—75 days
Buttercup—105 days
Early Golden Summer Crookneck—53 days
Fordhook® Zucchini—57 days, our favorite summer squash
Pumpkin
Small Sugar—100 days, for pies
Triple Treat—110 days, for pies, storage and hull-less seeds
Vegetable Spaghetti
Waltham Butternut—85 days
White Patty Pan—54 days

Tomatoes
    Burpee's Jubilee—72 days, orange
    ★ Burpee's Longkeeper—78 days, will store after picking
        6-12 weeks for winter eating
    Delicious—77 days, large fruits
    Red Cherry—72 days
    Roma VF—76 days, for sauce
    Yellow Pear—70 days
    Yellow Plum—70 days
Turnips
    Burpee's Purple-Top Yellow Rutabaga—90 days
    Purple-Top White Globe—55 days

USEFUL PLANTS

Mixed Bottle Gourds

FRUITS

Extra-dwarf fruit trees
    Garden Aprigold Apricot—5-6 feet
    Garden Bing Sweet Cherry—5-6 feet
    Garden Sun Peach—6-8 feet
    Golden Delicious Apple—5-6 feet
    Golden Glory Peach—4-5 feet
    Golden Prolific Nectarine—4-5 feet
    North Star Sour Cherry—8 feet
Apples
    Baldwin—standard
    Granny Smith—semi-dwarf and standard
    Grimes Golden—semi-dwarf
    Hyslop Crabapple
    continued

Salad-Burnet
(1/10 size)

> Jonathan—semi-dwarf and standard
> Red Delicious—semi-dwarf and standard
> Red McIntosh—semi-dwarf and standard
> Red Rome—semi-dwarf and standard
> Red Stayman Winesap—semi-dwarf and standard
> Yellow Delicious—semi-dwarf and standard
> Yellow Transparent—standard
> 5-in-1 includes Red Delicious, McIntosh, Stayman Winesap,
>   Yellow Delicious and Yellow Transparent

Apricots
> Chinese Golden—dwarf and standard
> Moorpark—dwarf and standard

Blackberries
> Darrow
> Thornfree

Blueberries
> Earliblue—early
> Blueray—midseason
> Bluecrop—midseason
> Berkeley—midseason
> Patriot—midseason
> Jersey—late
> Elliot—late

Rabbitseye Blueberries—for the South
> Tifblue—early
> Climax—early
> Garden Blue—early/midseason
> Woodard—midseason
> Southland—midseason/late

Boysenberries—thornless
Cherries
> Hansen's Bush
> Sour
>   Montmorancy
> Sweet
>   Bing
>   Black Tartarian
>   Kansas Sweet
>   Windsor
>   Yellow Glass

Elderberries
> Adams #2
> John's

Figs—everbearing

*Salsafy, or Vegetable
Oyster (1/3 size)*

Grapes
    Catawba
    Concord
    Muscadine—for the South
        Carlos
        Higgins
        Scuppernong
    Niagara
    Seedless
        Concord
        Himrod
        Interlaken
        Red Flame—for South
        Romulus

Marigold (Pot)
(1/20 size)

Peaches
    Belle of Georgia—dwarf and standard
    Early Elberta—dwarf
    Elberta—dwarf and standard
    Golden Jubilee—dwarf
    Hale Haven—dwarf and standard
    Red Haven—dwarf and standard
    Reliance—for cold climates, standard
Pears
    Bartlett—dwarf and standard
    Clapp's Favorite—dwarf
    Moonglow—standard
    Seckel—dwarf and standard
Persimmons
    Tanenashi
Plums
    American
        Monitor—standard
    European
        Fellenberg Italian Prune
        Mount Royal—hardiest, standard
        Shropshire Blue Damson—standard
        Stanley Prune—dwarf and standard
    Japanese
        Abundance—dwarf and standard
        Burbank—dwarf and standard

Raspberries
    Everbearing
        Black Treasure
        Fallgold — sweet, juicy, good yield, cold hardy ★
        Heritage
        Indian Summer
        September
    Standard — 4 selections
Strawberries
    Alpine — seeds and plants
    Everbearing
        Ogallala
        Ozark Beauty
        Shortcake
        Superfection
    Junebearing — 17 selections

NUTS

Almonds
    Hall's Hardy
Butternuts
Chinese Chestnuts
Filberts
    Barcelona
    Royal
Pecans
    Hardy Colby
    Hardy Northern
    Hardy Peruque
Walnuts
    Carpathian Strain English
    Thomas Black

*Large Bossin
Cabbage Lettuce
(1/6 size)*

FLOWERS

African Daisies
African Violets
    Rainbow Wonders
Alyssum — white (the most fragrant), rose, violet and red
Asters
    Burpee's Red Mound
    On Parade® — mixed colors and types
Begonias
Bulbs
    Bearded Iris — in all colors
    Dahlias — 27 selections, including Waterlily Dahlias

Gladiolas—22 selections, beautiful colors
Tuberous Begonias—28 selections
Calendula
Lemon Gem
Celosia—9 selections including Fire Dragon Plumed
Chrysanthemums—17 selections
Coleus—9 selections
Columbine
Dwarf Dragonfly
Giant Painted Daisies
Hollyhocks, Chater's Double
Deep Scarlet
Newport Rose
Rose
Yellow

Hyssop (1/12 size)

Marigolds
Fantastic
Marigolds are a Burpee specialty with 67 selections including
the Snowbird White, developed over many years as a
nationwide campaign
Nasturtiums
Crimson, golden, mahogany, yellow, orange, scarlet and
climbing varieties
Pansy
Orange Prince
Petunias—44 selections
Roses—20 selections
Everblooming Climbing
Roses—6 selections
Miniature Roses
Buttercup Yellow
Coral Pink
Cream
Lavender
Orange Red
Scarlet Red
White

Cherry Pepper (branch, 1/10;
fruit, 1/2 size)

Salvia—11 selections
Snapdragons—crimson, orange, rose, white, yellow
Stocks—Trysomic Seven Week in mixed colors

Strawflowers and Everlastings—excellent selection with good photos,
including:

Job's Tears	Starflowers
Lunaria	Statice—in a rainbow of colors
Quaking Grass	Xeranthemum
Ruby Grass	

continued

Adam's Early White Broccoli (1/10 size)

Broccoli

Broccoli is best started in a flat early in spring or fall and transplanted onto 15-inch centers. The leaves of broccoli are more nutritious than the heads. Pick the leaves as they mature, starting with the lower ones and cook like cabbage. In 10 square feet, broccoli will yield 4-5 pounds of heads and 8-11 pounds of leaves.

• TIPS FROM THE TOP OF THE WORLD •

continued
Sweet Peas—another Burpee specialty
Tithonia
      Mexican Sunflower—a real show stopper
Verbena
Wildflower Mixes
      Burpee's American
      Midwest
      Southeast
Zinnias—51 selections
      Button Box dwarf—10 inches high
      Cut and Come Again—mixed colors
      Envy—green flowers
      Old Mexico

ORNAMENTALS

Blackhawk Mountain Ash
Burning Bush
Bush Honeysuckle
Butterfly Bush—our neighbor planted these instead of building a
    fence; quite effective, vigorous and attractive
Clematis—gorgeous flowers, 11 selections
    including Star of India and Prince Philip
Crape Myrtle
Crimson King Maple
Dogwoods—3 kinds
Double Mock Orange—beautiful scent
Ferns
        Christmas
        Maidenhair
        Ostrich
Flowering Crabapples—6 kinds
French Blue Hydrangea
French Pink Pussywillow
Gold Forsythia
Golden Chain Tree
Golden Rain Tree
Jack-in-the-Pulpit
Lombardy Poplar
Mountain Ash
Norway Maple—golden yellow leaves in autumn
Oregon Grape Holly
Paul's Scarlet Hawthorne
Persian Lilac
Pink Flowering Almond
Purple Wisteria
Rose Tree of China
Star Magnolia
Sugar Maple—orange, gold and scarlet leaves in autumn
Trumpet Vine
Weeping Japanese Cherry
Wisconsin Weeping Maple
Yellow Trumpet Vine
Yucca

Beauregard Lettuce
(1/6 size)

GROUND COVERS

Lily of the Valley
Penngift Crownvetch—grows even in semi-shade
Vinca—Periwinkle

TOOLS AND SUPPLIES

Berry Baskets
Berry Screen
Cherry Pitter
Earthworms
Fruit Picker
Garden Stool
Grape Spiral
Havahart Traps—2 kinds
Japanese Beetle Trap
Jelly Strainer
Knee-pads
Ladybugs
Minimum/Maximum Thermometer
Mole Trap
Onion Bags
Praying Mantis Egg Cases
Pressure Canners
Pumpkin Screen
Rain Gauges
Rotenone
Tanglefoot
Thuricide
Victorio Strainer
Wire Mesh Harvest Basket

*Long-fruited Green Okra (seed-vessels
1/3 size)*

*Large Green
Paris Artichoke
(1/3 size)*

Early Seed and Garden Centre
2615 Lorne Ave.
Saskatoon, Sask. S7J-0S5 Canada

Early is an old family-held seed company. They are a good source of seed grains and forage, also offering a complete standard selection of flowers and vegetables, especially those that do well in the North.

VEGETABLES

Asparagus
   Viking
Beans
   11 snap beans
   Exhibition Long Pod—Broad Bean
   Green—3 bush varieties
   Romano bush
   Royal Burgundy
   Yellow—3 bush varieties
Beets—4 kinds including Cylindra
Cabbage Family
   Broccoli—Green Sprouting Calabrese
   Brussels Sprouts—Long Island Improved
   Cabbage—9 selections
         Houston Evergreen—stores well
   Cauliflower—Super Snowball
Carrots—8 selections
   Little Finger—for tub planting
   Paris Market—gourmet
Celeriac
   Large Smooth Prague
Celery
   Golden Self Blanching
   Utah (Green)
Citron

Perennial Lettuce
(1/8 size;
detached leaf,
1/3 size)

Corn—all early varieties, 60-75 days to maturity
   Dorinny
   Early Golden Bantam
   Gill's Early Golden Market
Cucumbers
   Early Russian—for pickling
   Mincu
   National Pickling
   Straight Eight

Greens
    Chard
        Lucullus
        Rhubarb
    Endive
        Green Curled
    Spinach
        Bloomsdale
        King of Denmark
Leek
    London Flag
Lettuce — 8 selections
Mangels
    Giant Sugar Rose
Melons
    Cantaloupe — Far North
    Watermelon — small short-season types
        Early Canada
        New Hampshire Midget
        Sugar Baby
Onions
    Bunching
        Annual Green
        Silver Queen
    Globe — 4 selections

Green Purslane (1/8 size; detached branch, 1/3 size)

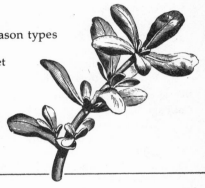

Brussels Sprouts

Brussels Sprouts grow best where they have 4 months of cool weather. Start in flats and transplant onto 18-inch centers. For best results, break off leaves by pulling downward as each node develops on the main stem (just about the leaf junction). Yield for 10 square feet is 10-14 pounds.

Dwarf Brussels Sprouts (1/10 size)

• TIPS FROM THE TOP OF THE WORLD •

The Seed Finder

Onions continued
- Sets
  - Multipliers
  - Yellow Dutch

Parsnips
- Guernsey
- Hollow Crown

Peas
- China Snow—edible podded
- Freezer 69
- Green Arrow
- Homesteader
- Laxton's Progress
- Little Marvel
- Strategem Improved
- Sugar Snap

Peppers
- Golden Bell—sweet
- Red Cherry—sweet

Potatoes
- Kennebec—white
- Netted Gem
- Norland—red
- Pontiac—red
- Warba—white round
- Waseca—red

Radish—white, red, pink and black types—9 selections

Squash—9 selections
- Pumpkins—3 selections
  - King of Mammoths—up to 100 pounds
- Show King—gigantic

Tomatoes—all early maturing for cold climates
- Bounty
- Brookpact
- Bush Beefsteak
- Earliana
- Early Chatham
- Manitoba
- Starfire
- Sub-Arctic
- Swift

Rollisson's Telegraph Cucumber (1/5 size)

"Rose de Malaga" Sweet Potato (1/8 size)

Late Flat Dutch
Drumhead Cabbage
(1/12 size)

Cabbage

There are many cabbages to choose from: smaller spring varieties, large autumn ones, the crinkly savoys and storage heads. Stokes offers over 40 varieties. Red cabbages are less attractive to the green cabbage-worms and can be sold at market for a slightly higher price. Transplant seedlings onto 15-inch centers, the largest varieties onto 18-inch centers. Yield is 19-38 pounds from 10 square feet.

• TIPS FROM THE TOP OF THE WORLD •

continued

FLOWERS

All the standards from Ageratum to Zinnia including:
    Arabis-Rock Cress
    California Poppies—mixed colors
    Chrysanthemum—single and double from seed
    Climbing Flowers
        Canary Bird Vine
        Cardinal Climber
        Cobaca—Cup and Saucer Vine
        Scarlet Runner Bean
    Cosmos
        Dazzler
        Early Sensation
        Sunset
    Hollyhock
        Chater's Double
        Indian Spring
    Marigolds—10 of the best selections
    Queen Anne's Lace
    Shasta Daisies
    Tulip Poppies

FORAGE

Alfalfa—all kinds
Brome
Clover—all types
Pasture Mixes
Rye Grass
Sanfoin
Timothy
Trefoil
Wheat Grass

GRAINS

Barley—3 selections
Buckwheat
Durum Wheat
Faba Beans
Field Corn
Flax—2 selections
Lentils
Millet
Oats—3 selections
Peas—Century-Trapper
Rapeseed—7 selections
Spring and Fall Rye
Spring Wheat
    —3 selections
Winter Wheat

Sage (1/8 size)

*Large Tours Pumpkin
(1/6 size)*

EARLY SEED AND GARDEN CENTRE

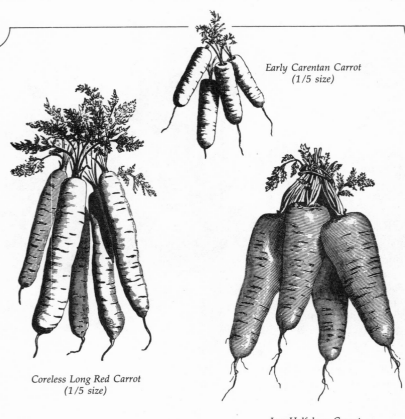

Early Carentan Carrot
(1/5 size)

Coreless Long Red Carrot
(1/5 size)

Luc Half-long Carrot
(1/5 size)

Carrots

Carrots are often hard to germinate. They need to be kept moist for up to 3 weeks and covered only very lightly. We often place a piece of chicken wire with a 2-inch mesh over the soil to help space seeds evenly. We just drop 2 seeds in each space. Seeds can also be broadcast. Use 1 level teaspoon of seed for 10 square feet. Practicing on paper first helps. Only half the seed normally germinates. If you are not there to make sure soil stays moist you can cover the bed with a moist piece of burlap. Check underneath daily for germination and remove burlap to give them light and air once they are started. Tamping the soil over the seeds firmly also aids germination. Plant carrots 2-3 inches apart. Yield is 15-30 pounds from 10 square feet. The sweetest carrots are grown in moderate weather, neither too hot nor cold. Heavy clay or rocky soils grow shorter varieties. Two good sources of carrot seed are Abundant Life and Stokes.

Epicure Seeds
Box 69
Avon, NY 14414

Epicure Seeds is a relatively new company. The catalog reviews and offers the best of what is available from older European seed houses that emphasize gourmet flavor and quality.

VEGETABLES AND HERBS

Basil
>Genovese Verde Senz 'Aromad'—mint-scented from Italy
>Piccolo Verde Fino—for Pesto

Chard
>Ampuis Swiss from France

Corn Salad

Curly Endive

Lettuce—especially those resistant to heat or cold
>All the Year Round Butterhead—from England and many more
>Patience Butterhead—from Belgium
>Reine des Glaces Loosehead—from France
>Zomerkoning Butterhead—from Holland

Parsley
>Clivi—aromatic, from Belgium
>Gigante de Italia—pungent, from Italy
>Multikrul—cold resistant, from Holland

Peas
>Carouby de Mausanne Sugar Pea—from France
>Relavil Petit Pois—tasty, early dwarf, from France

Peppers
>Di Napoli Green—pungent flavor for cooking and pickling, from Italy
>Manto Green Bell—from Holland

Spinach
>Estivato d'Ete—good flavor, long harvest, slow bolter, from Belgium

Tomatoes
>Alicante—for broiling, from England

Black-seeded All-the-Year-Round
Cabbage Lettuce
(scale not shown)

Exotica Seed Company
1742 Laurel Canyon Road
West Hollywood, CA 90046

This company specializes in exotic fruits, mostly of tropical origin (Hawaii, Mexico, South America and Asia). Offerings are mostly suited to Southern California, Arizona, and New Mexico with a few choice selections for high mountain climates and even some little used fruits for colder regions. Plant descriptions are knowledgeable and reliable for regions where plants will grow well. Descriptions of flavor are refreshingly honest. Many tropicals can be grown in colder climates in greenhouses.

FRUITS

Carob—beautiful round tree with glossy foliage. 6-inch pods are chocolate colored and drop in great abundance for 3-4 months of the year. We like to chew on the pods and our goats go crazy over them.

Cherimoya

Cherry Plums

Chicle—sap is the main ingredient of Chiclets Gum

Guavas

Jujube

Kiwi

Loquats—fruit is about one-half seed, flavor is like apricot. Very abundant. With fig, loquat and persimmon one could have fruit nearly year round.

Mulberries—so easy to grow, prolific and delicious

Natal Plums

Papaya

Paw Paw

Persimmons, Fuyu—fruits have none of the usual astringency of persimmons

Pitaya—large cactus produces large fruit tasting like fig

Pomegranate

Pond Apple

Prickly Pears—a desert-growing cactus. We've seen them growing as a formidable fence with good tasting fruit.

Raisin Tree

Sapote—hardy tree produces abundance of fruits with custard-like texture

Soursop

Strawberry Tree

Tahitian Melon Squash

Tamarind
        and many others

Henry Field Seed and Nursery Co.
407 Sycamore Ave.
Shenandoah, IA 51602

Fields is an all-round, old-time source of just about everything; vegetables, some flowers, fruit trees, berries, and ornamental plants. Their selection of flowering shrubs and vines is great and they offer the Turnbull Giant Pear, a chance backyard discovery with fruit that tastes like an apple when young and a pear later. Good deals on bulk gladiola bulbs. They emphasize varieties for hot midwest summers.

VEGETABLES

Artichokes
    Globe—roots
    Jerusalem—tubers
Asparagus—from roots or seed

Beans
    Dried
        Black Turtle
        Garbanzo
        Great White Northern
        Horticultural Dwarf Taylor
        Pinquito—small pink
        Pinto
        Red Kidney
        White Navy
    Fava
    Lima
        Speckled Calico
    Mung—for sprouts
    Pole Winged
    Snap
        Asparagus Yard Long
        Cherokee Wax Yellow Bush
        Daisy Bush—pods held above leaves
        Purple Pod Pole
        Royal Burgundy Pole
        Tendergreen Bush—no strings or fiber
    Soy
        Prize Edible—85 days

Beets

Soup Celery
(1/6 size)

Albino White	Dark Red Canner	Mammoth Long Red
Badger's Baby	Giant Western Sugar	Mangel—for livestock
Cylindra	Golden	

Cabbage Family
    Broccoli
        Spartan Early—frost resistant
    Cabbage
        Baby Head—69 days
        Chieftain Mammoth Savoy—88 days
        Goliath—Zwaan Jumbo—105 days, up to 25 pounds
        Premium Late Dutch—good storer, 105 days
    Collards
        Vates
Carrots
    Baby Nantes
    Glowing Ball—round nugget shape
    Gold-Pak—sweet and juicy
    Lady Finger—gourmet type
    Tendersweet

Corn
    Broomcorn
    Hickory King—for hominy
    Indian Corn—ornamental
    Reid's Yellow Dent
    Strawberry Popcorn
    Trucker's Delight

Green Bush Basil
(1/8 size)

Cucumbers
    Armenian
    Baby Mincu—for pickling whole,
        good tub plant
    Bushcrop
    Lemon
    National Pickle
    Straight Eight
    Table Green
Garlic
    California White
    Elephant
Jicama
Lettuce
    Black Seeded Simpson
    Buttercrunch
    Chicken—for poultry feed
    Salad Bowl
    Slo-bolt—45 days
    Sweetie—40 days

Angelica
(scale not shown)

Melons
   Bananas—novelty
   Cantaloupes

Broad-leaved Garden Cress
(1/5 size)

      Big Daddy
      Field's Giant—up to 14 pounds
      Golden Honey
      Hale's Best
      Hearts of Gold
      Honey Rock
      Iroquois
      Rocky Ford
   Watermelons
      Cobb Gem—up to 125 pounds
      Crimson Sweet—good keeper, good flavor
      Field's Fourth of July Northern Sweet—70 days
      Midget Sugar Baby
      Sugar Bush—80 days
      Tendersweet—orange yellow flesh

Mushroom Spawn
Okra
   Clemson Spineless
   Dwarf Green Long Pod
   Dwarf Lee
   Emerald Green Velvet
   Red

Onions
   Debutante—very mild white
   Owa—a yellow torpedo type
   Red Mac
   Red Torpedo
   Southport—large red globe
   Walla Walla—giant sweet
   White Bermuda
   White Portugal—pickling size
   White Sweet Spanish
   Yellow Sweet Spanish

Apple-shaped Celeriac
(1/6 size)

Peas
   Early Snap Bush—58 days
   Extra Early Alaska—56 days
   Southern
      Black-eyed Cowpea—60 days
      Mississippi Silver Brown Crowder—60 days
      Pink Eye Purple Hull—50 days
      Zipper Cream—75 days
   Sparkle—59 days, 18 inches high
   Wando—heat tolerant

Peppers
 Hot
  Anaheim
  Cayenne
  Hungarian Yellow Wax
  Jalapeno
  Pepperoncini
  Red Chili
  Serrano—the hottest!
 Sweet
  Keystone Resistant Giant Green
  King of the North—65 days,
   for short seasons
  Pimento Select
Potatoes—seed potato sets
 Kennebec
 McNeilly Everbearing
 Norgold Russet
 Norland
 Red Pontiac
 Russet Burbank
 White Cobbler
Potatoes, sweet
 All Gold
 Centennial
 Nancy Hall
 Vardaman—bush
 Vineless Porto Rico

*Purple Sprouting, or Asparagus,
Broccoli (1/8 size;
detached portion,
natural size)*

Radishes
 Chinese Rose—pink, 50 days
 Crimson Giant—28 days
 Field's German Giant Red—29 days
 French Breakfast—25 days
 Giant White Globe—28 days
 Hailstone—large, white, round, 28 days
 Long White Icicle—27 days
 ★Tendersweet Red Prince—24 days
Rhubarb
 Chipman's Canada Red—sweet
 Crimson Cherry—tart
 Flare
 Victoria Tenderstalk
Shallots
Spinach
 Dixie Market—38 days
 Giant Nobel—43 days

*Flat Tripoli Onion
(1/3 size)*

Squash
    Delicata Sweet Potato Squash—95 days
    Giant Show King—110 days, up to 300 pounds
    Jumbo Pink Banana—105 days
    Naked Seeded—seeds do not have husks
    Pumpkins
        Big Max
        Big Moon—up to 200 pounds
    Striped Cushaw—large crookneck pumpkin
    Vegetable Spaghetti

Tomatoes
    Jubilee—Golden Sunray
    Snowball—white
    Sweetie—cherry-type
    Yellow Pear
Turnips
    White Egg—50 days

USEFUL PLANTS

Gourds—3 mixtures plus
    Birdhouse
    Dipper
    Luffa sponge
Tobacco
    Burley No. 21, mild white

Oval Yellow China, or Robin's Egg,
Kidney Bean
(1/8 size)

FRUITS

Cold hardy varieties are stressed.

Apples
    Anoka—standard
    Chieftain—winter hardy, dwarf and standard
    Cortland—standard
    Criterion Golden—dwarf
    Delcon—semi-dwarf
    Eve's Delight—giant fruit, dwarf
    Granny Smith—dwarf and standard
    Grimes Golden—standard
    Haralson—standard and dwarf
    Jonathan—dwarf and standard
    Lodi—dwarf and standard
    McIntosh—dwarf and standard
    Northwest Greening—standard
    Red Delicious—dwarf and standard

continued

Cauliflower

Cauliflower plants provide a wonderful surprise since most of their heading occurs only in a few days. Try purple varieties as well as white. Redwood City Seed Company carries a tropical variety, Snowpeak, that produces in summer. Transplant seedlings onto 15-inch centers. Yield is 10-20 pounds from 10 square feet.

Lenormand's
Short-stalked Cauliflower
(1/10 size)

• TIPS FROM THE TOP OF THE WORLD •

Apples continued
>   Red Winesap—standard and dwarf
>   Seek-No-Further—dwarf
>   Summer Granny—standard
>   Whitney Crab—standard
>   Yellow Delicious—dwarf and standard
>   5-in-1 includes Yellow Delicious, McIntosh, Grimes Golden,
>   Jonathan and Red Delicious

Apricots
>   "Bush" Manchurian
>   Early Golden—standard
>   Goldcot—frost resistant, standard or dwarf
>   Hardy Iowa—standard
>   Henderson—standard
>   Moorpark—dwarf

Blackberries
>   Black Satin—thornless
>   Darrow
>   Dirksen Thornless—early
>   Snyder—hardy

Blueberries—4 varieties, all hybrids

Boysenberries
>   Giant Thornless

Buffalo Berries

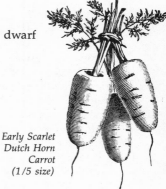

Early Scarlet
Dutch Horn
Carrot
(1/5 size)

Cherries—standard unless noted otherwise
    Bing—sweet
    Black Tartarian—sweet
    Bush Cherries
        Hansen's Sweet—purple
        Nanking Red—tart
        South Dakota Ruby Sweet
    Early Richmond—sour
    Golden—sweet
    Kansas—sweet
    Montmore—sour
    Montmorency—sour
    North Star—dwarf
    Stella—sweet
    Sweet Delight—black
    Wild Black
Chokecherries
Currants
    Red Lake
    Wilder
Dewberries
    Lucretia
Elderberries
Gooseberries
Grapes
    Buffalo—blue
    Canadice Red Seedless
    Catawba—dark copper
    Concord—purple
    Fredonia—hardy, early
    Himrod Golden Seedless
    Interlaken Seedless—light green
    Muscadine—for southern climates
        Bronze Scuppernong
        Southland—blue
    Niagara—white
    Portland—white early
    Red Caco
    Seedless Concord
    Steuben—blue, hardy
Huckleberries
Nectarines
    Hardired—standard
    Mericrest—dwarf
    Surecrop—standard
Pawpaw

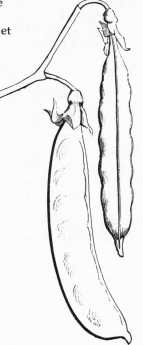

*Pods of Early Dwarf
Brittany Sugar Pea*

Peaches
    Belle of Georgia—standard
    Bonanza—dwarf
    Elberta Yellow Freestone—dwarf and standard
    Hale Haven—early freestone, dwarf and standard
    Polly—"white," hardy, dwarf and standard
    Red Haven—early, hardy, dwarf and standard
    Reliance—hardy, standard
    White Champion—standard
    Wisconsin Balmer—standard

Pears—standard unless otherwise noted
    Bartlett—also as dwarf
    Colette
    Duchess—dwarf only
    Kieffer
    Max Red Bartlett
    Maxine
    Moonglow—also as dwarf
    Seckel
    Turnbull Giant—young fruit
        tastes like apple, when ripe
        like pear
    5-in-1

Winter Purslane
(1/4 size)

Persimmon—hardy native type
Plums
    All red
    Blue Damson
    Green Gage
    Ozark Premier
    Santa Rosa
    Stanley Prune—also as dwarf
    Superior—also as dwarf
    Underwood
    Waneta
Plumcot
    Parfait
Plum-Peach cross

Raspberries
    August Red   Hilton—red
    Black Hawk   Jewel Black
    Cumberland—black   Liberty—red
    Fall Gold   Purple Sodus
    Fallred   Southland—red
    Heritage—red, sweet   Tayberry—purple

Serviceberries
Strawberries—Everbearing
        Fort Laramie—heat and cold hardy
        Ogallala
        Ozark Beauty
        Sunburst—good yields
        Sweet Delight
Wineberries

NUT TREES

Almond
        Hall's Hardy
Butternut
Chinese Chestnut
English Walnut
Hazelnut
Pecan
        Colby
        Giant Mahan
        Major
        Stuart
Shellbark Hickory

*Early Dwarf Purple
Eggplant
(1/10 size)*

ORNAMENTALS

Dwarf Banana Plant
Flowering Bulbs—dahlias, gladiolas, lilies (including Lily of the Valley)
Flowering Vines
Flowering shrubs and hedge plants too numerous to list
Flowers—many kinds in inexpensive packets
        Begonias
        Chinese Balloon Flower
        Chinese Lanterns
        Lupines
        Oriental Poppies
        Painted Daisy
Lawn Mixtures
        Baron Bluegrass—fast sodmaker
        Bentgrass
        100% Bluegrass Mix
        Joy Kentucky Bluegrass—heat tolerant
        Park Kentucky Bluegrass—rapid starting
        Playground Turf
        Regal Turf
        Sun and Shade
        Zoysia Plugs

*Dwarf
Wrinkled Pea
(1/10 size)*

continued

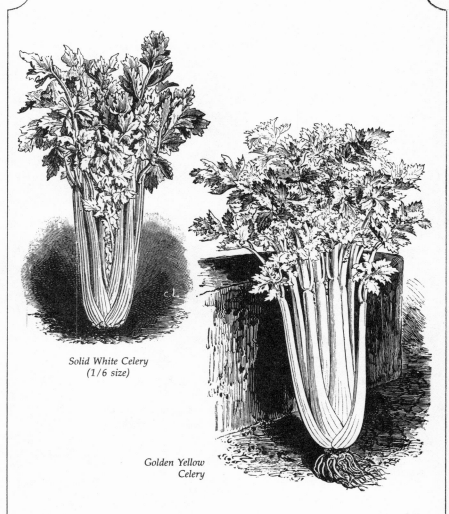

Solid White Celery
(1/6 size)

Golden Yellow
Celery

Celery

Celery takes a long time to mature. We have the best results growing seedlings in flats 6 inches deep. After several months, when seedlings are 6-9 inches high, transplant into growing beds on 6-inch centers. Yields as high as 48-96 pounds are possible from 10 square feet. Fordhook® celery from Burpee is a good all-round variety. Start celery very early.

Ornamentals continued

Roses Galore including miniatures (10 inches high) — light green, red, yellow/pink/red, lavender, orange, red and white stripes

Trees
  Austrian Pine
  Birch — 4 kinds
  Colorado Blue Spruce
  Maples — 9 kinds
  Norway Spruce
  Red Cedar
  Red Oak
  Scotch Pine
  Sugar Maple
  Weeping Willow

GARDEN ACCESSORIES

Barnyard Fly Parasites
Bone Meal
Cherry Pitter
Corn Cutter
Fish Emulsion
Fish Meal
Grasshopper Spore
Green Lacewings
"Hard to Crack" Nutcracker
Havahart Small Animal Traps
Lady Bugs
Milky Spore — for grub control
"Nee" Guards
Nitragin Bean Inoculant
Praying Mantis
Square Sprinklers
Tree Tanglefoot
Tricogamma Wasps
Wooden Garden Labels
Worms

Broad, or London,
Flag Leek

White Curled Swiss Chard (1/10 size)

Chard

Swiss Chard is a great producer of greens and a year-round standby in our garden. Chard grows as white, green, gold and red-ribbed varieties. The last is called Rhubarb Chard, a popular type for edible landscaping. Plant seeds on 8-inch centers. Yield is about 40 pounds or more from 10 square feet. It makes an excellent green food for goats and chickens. We also dry leaves and crumble them over pizza and other foods.

——————————— • TIPS FROM THE TOP OF THE WORLD • ———————————

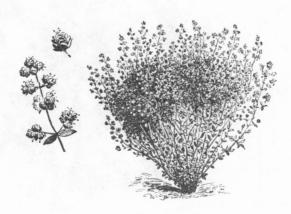

Sweet, or Annual, Marjoram
(scale not shown)

Gurney's Seed and Nursery Co.
Yankton, SD 57079

Gurney's is an old-time seed company with a giant colorful catalog full of a little of everything: vegetables, flowers, shade trees, fruit trees, hedges, and so on. The personal testimonials are classic. They offer some good inexpensive deals on many items if you use discrimination.

VEGETABLES

Artichokes
    Globe
    Jerusalem

Asparagus
    Roberts
    Waltham

Beans
    Dried

Black-eyed	Pinto
Black Turtle	Red
Dwarf Horticultural Taylor	Red Kidney
Garbanzo	Soldier
Great Northern White	Soybean—Disoy Edible
Navy White	Swedish Brown
Pink Chili	

    Favas
    Flamata Flageolot—similar to Limas
    Limas
        King of the Garden—Pole
        Thorogreen Baby Bush
    Snap
        Blue Lake—Bush and Pole
        Daisy Bush—sets pods above leaves
        Earliana Bush
        Kentucky Wonder—Bush and Pole
        Purple Pod
        Romano—Italian, Bush and Pole
        Royal Burgundy
        Stringless Green Pod
        Tenderette
        Top Crop

Beets

Baby Canning	Honey Red—sweet
Cylindra	Sugar Beets
Golden	

Early Carentan Carrot (1/5 size)

Cabbage
    Babyhead
    Danish Ballhead
    Gurney's Giant—20-35 lbs.
    Late Flat Dutch
    Mammoth Red Rock
    and others
Carrots
    Early Coreless
    Glowing Ball
    Tendersweet
    The "Carrot Stick"
    and others
Cauliflower
    Self-Blanch
    Stovepipe—heat tolerant
Corn
    Black Mexican
    Country Gentleman
    Golden Bantam
    Hickory King
    Midget—for patio boxes
    Ornamental
        Broomcorn
        Purple Husk
        Rainbow
    Popcorn
        Black
        Calico—multi-colored
        Dynamite
        Japanese White Hull-less
        South American Yellow
        Strawberry
    Stowell's Evergreen
Cucumbers
    Armenian Yard Long
    Bush Crop
    Everbearing Pickling
    Gherkin Pickling
    Lemon
    White Wonder
Endive
    French
    Leaf
Ginger Roots

Magdeburg Chicory
(1/5 size)

Finocchio, or Florence, Fennel
(1/5 size)

Horseradish—crowns and cuttings
Jicama
Lettuce
     Chicken—fodder
     Continuity Extra Early Head—73 days.
     Ithaca—heat resistant Head type
     Prize-head—beautiful green leaves with reddish edges
     Ruby Red Leaf
     Sweetie—does not get bitter
Mangels
     Mammoth Long Red Fodder
Melons
     Cantaloupes
          Bush
          Far North
          Gurney's Sweet Perfection
          Honeyrock—sweet
          Kazaki—white fleshed
          Minnesota Midget
          Rock Ford—green fleshed
     Honeyloupe—Honeydew and Cantaloupe cross
     Watermelons
          Black Diamond—round, up to 40 pounds
          Cobb Gem—up to 130 pounds
          Congo—up to 40 pounds, sweet
          Early Canada—up to 15 pounds
          Golden Midget—yellow outside, red inside
          King and Queen—good winter keeper
          Market Midget—69 days, 3-5 pounds
          Northern Sweet—70 days, up to 15 pounds
          Sugar Bush—80 days, up to 6 pounds
          Tendersweet—orange yellow flesh
Okra
     Red
Onions
     He-Shi-Ko Perennial
     Pearl Cocktail
     Red Torpedo
     Slicing—long white
Peanuts
     Early Spanish No. 1—100 days
Peas
     Extra Early Alaska Pole
     Frost-Bite Pole—frost resistant
     Gray Sugar Dwarf

Orache
(1/30
size)

continued

Collards (1/12 size)

Collards

Collards are probaby the best nutritional bargain. They contain as much protein and many times the calcium as an equal amount of milk, though you cannot eat big quantities of collards. We especially like them with potatoes. Try mashed potatoes, cooked collards and onions made into a giant pancake. Collards will grow nearly year-round, though they prefer cooler weather, growing when few other vegetables are available. Transplant seedlings onto 12-inch centers. Ten square feet will yield 19-38 pounds.

— • TIPS FROM THE TOP OF THE WORLD • —

Peas continued
> Green Arrow Bush
> Little Marvel Semi-dwarf
> Mammoth Melting Sugar Pole
> Novella Leafless
> Sugar Mel Early Sugar Snap
> Sugar Rae Sugar Snap—highest yielding
> Soup varieties
>> Black-eyed
>> Brown Crowder
>> Purple Hull—Pink-eyed
> Wando
> White Sugar Dwarf

*Superfine
Early Cabbage
(scale not shown)*

Peppers
- Cubanelle Sweet Italian—yellow green
- Hungarian Yellow Hot
- Jalepeno Hot
- Mexican Chilis
    - Anaheim
    - Ancho
    - Fresno
    - Hot Large Red Cherry
    - Numex Big Jim
    - Pepperoncini
    - Red Chili
    - Santa Fe Grande
    - Serrano
- Paprika
- Pimento, Spartan Garnet—sweet
- Red Cayenne Hot

*Large Yellow Lentil
(1/10 size;
detached branch,
natural size)*

Potatoes
- Blue
- Butte Russet—up to 20% more protein
- Explorer White Potato Seed
- Irish Cobbler
- Kennebec
- Lady Finger German
- New Norland
- Norgold Russet
- Red Pontiac
- Sweet Potatoes—3 varieties
- Viking

Radishes
- Firecracker Red
- Japanese Daikon
- Mr. Big
- Parat German Giant
- White Prince

Rhubarb
- Flare
- Valentine

Salsify
- Black
- White

*Paris Market-Garden Melon
(1/5 size)*

Squash
    Early Butternut
    Gold Rush—golden zucchini
    Golden Nugget Acorn
    Hercules Butternut
    Hungarian Mammoth Winter—up to
        150 pounds
    Jumbo Pink Banana—10-35 pounds
    Pumpkins
        Atlantic Giant—up to 450 pounds
        Big Max—up to 100 pounds
        Big Moon—up to 200 pounds
        Cinderella Bush
        Little Boo—small white-skinned
        Naked Seeded
        Small Sugar—for pies
        Triple Delight—for pies, jack o' lanterns plus hull-less seeds
        Winter Luxury—one of the sweetest
    Table Ace Bush Winter
    Vegetable Spaghetti
    Warted Hubbard—up to 12 pounds
Shallots
Tomatoes
    Campbell's 1327
    Climbing—10-15 foot plants
    Golden Delight Early
    Gurney's Cold Set—65 days,
        frost resistant
    Royal Chico—for ketchup
    Stakeless—thick stemmed
    Sub-Arctic—45 days
    White Beauty
    Yellow Pear

Tansy (1/20 size)

OTHER USEFUL PLANTS

Comfrey
Grain Amaranth
Gourds
    Penguin, Birdhouse,
        Dipper and others
Hops
Jojoba
Luffa
Sorghum—makes a
    sweet syrup

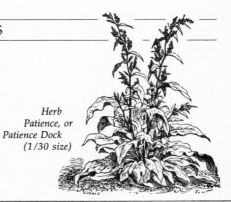

*Herb
Patience, or
Patience Dock
(1/30 size)*

FRUITS

Most fruit trees carried by Gurney are super hardy and suitable for growing in colder northern climates.

Apples
      Anoka
      Cortland
      Fireside
      Haralson
      Honeygold
      Lodi
      McIntosh
      Northwest Greening
      Prairie Spy
      Red Baron
      Red Duchess
      Red June
      Wealthie
      Wolf River—100-year-old
        variety
      and others
         8 dwarfs
         3 crabapples
         and a 5-in-1 tree

Malta, or Ice,
Drumhead Lettuce
(1/6 size)

Apricots
      5 hardy types including the super hardy Manchurian Bush—
        said to withstand -50°F to 110°+F
      Dwarf Moorpark
      Goldcot
      Manchu
      Moongold
      Scout
      Sungold
Cherries
      Bing
      Black Tartarian
      Early Montmore
      Meteor—semi-dwarf
      Montmorency—for pies
      North Star—hardy dwarf
      Royal Ann
      Stella Sweet—self-fertile

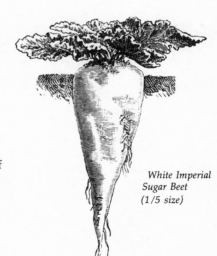

White Imperial
Sugar Beet
(1/5 size)

continued

continued

Fig
    Brown Turkey
Grapes and Berries
    Blackberries
        Black Satin Thornfree
        Darrow
        Ebony King
    Blueberries
        Saskatoon
        Tophat
    Boysenberries — thornless

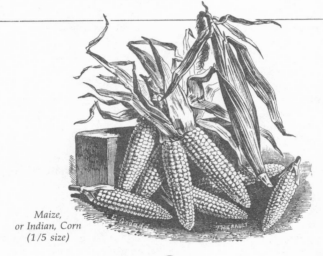

*Maize,
or Indian, Corn
(1/5 size)*

Corn

The most important thing about corn is to plant in blocks of at least 16 plants and not a long row. Corn is pollinated by the wind. Pollen from the top tassels must reach the silks. Each silk leads to one kernel. If an ear does not fill out properly it is because some kernels did not get pollinated. If you are limited to small plantings, you can shake or brush pollen from the tassels onto the silks. Ample space should be left between corn varieties or you can get ears with mixed kernels. Open-pollinated corn is planted on 15-inch centers. Ten square feet will produce 3-7 pounds of shelled undried corn. We leave the suckers, or side shoots, on for extra ears. Though sometimes tiny, they can be delicious. Strawberry Popcorn makes pretty strawberry-shaped ears.

Currants
    Red Lake
    Wilder
Dewberries
Elderberries
Gooseberries
    Pixwell
    Welcome
Grapes
    Beta—hardy wild grape
    Concord
    Edelweiss—hardy to -30°F
    Fredonia
    Himrod
    Niagara
    Steuben
    Swenson Red—hardy to -30°F
Raspberries
    Black Hawk
    Canby
    Cumberland
    Fall Gold
    Fall Red
    Giant Newburgh
    Heritage
    Indian Summer
    John Robertson
    Latham
    September Red
Strawberries
    Everbearing
        Gem
        Ogallala
        Streamliner
        Superfection
    Junebearing
        Cyclone
        Dunlap
        Earlidawn
        Guardian
        Sparkle
        Trumpeter
Mulberries
Nectarines
    Mericrest

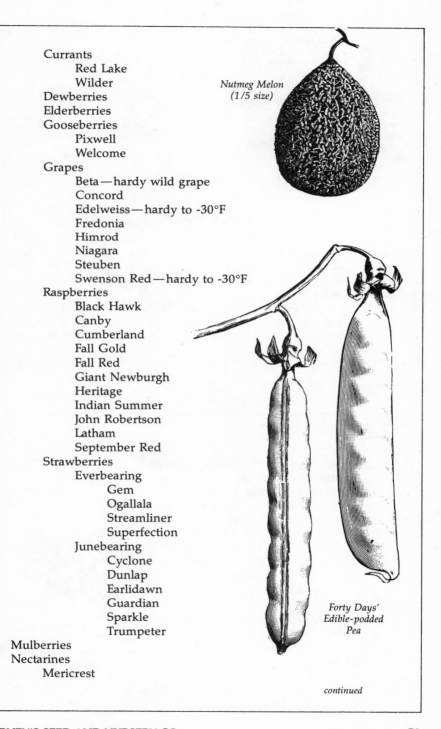

Nutmeg Melon
(1/5 size)

Forty Days'
Edible-podded
Pea

continued

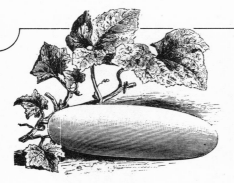

Early Yellow Dutch Cucumber
(1/5 size)

Snake Cucumber
(1/15 size)

Cucumbers

Cucumbers need lots of moisture and warmth. Sunnybrook is a good standard variety. Lemon cucumbers are a real treat when picked young (yellowish white in color). We especially like Armenian cucumbers. They are a pale green and are often long, thin and slightly curved. The flavor, crunch and coolness are all there, though they are easier to grow—more drought resistant. They are hardly ever bitter or prickly. Skins are thin and edible. Cucumber seedlings should be transplanted onto 12-inch centers. Yields are 31-58 pounds from 10 square feet.

• TIPS FROM THE TOP OF THE WORLD •

continued
Paw Paw
Peaches—standard unless otherwise noted
      Elberta—also as dwarf
      Hale Haven—also as dwarf
      Polly—"The Eskimo", also as dwarf
      Reliance—also as dwarf
      Sun Haven
      Valiant
Pears
      Douglas   Lincoln
      Giant Bartlett   Maxine
      Kieffer   5-in-1
Persimmon—native type
Plums—good hardy types
Quince
      Champion
      Pineapple
Fruit Cocktail Tree—4-in-1 graft of apricot, peach, nectarine and plum

Common, French, or Narrow-leaved Thyme (1/8 size; detached sprig, 1/2 size)

NUT TREES

Almond
     Hall's Hardy
Butternut
Chinese Chestnut
Hazelnut
     American
Hickory
Pecan
     Hardy
     Stuart
Walnut
     Black
     Hardy English
     Thomas Black

*Gherkin, or Pickling, Cucumber
(young fruit)*

FLOWERS

Too numerous to list. More unusual are:
     Chippendale Daisy
     Gas Plant
     Inexpensive gladiolas and other bulbs
     Many roses of all types
     Perennial Foxglove
     Prairie Flower Mix

Chardon Potato

ORNAMENTALS

Hedges and shrubs from Lilac to Pussy Willow, Butterfly Bush
  to Wisteria
Indoor Dwarf Fruits
    Banana
    Dancy Tangerine
    Fig
    Lemon
    Lime
    Otaheite Orange
Shade Trees from Ash to Dawn Redwood
Windbreak seedings—all kinds, very inexpensive

TOOLS AND GARDEN AIDS

Bird Net—keeps birds from vulnerable plants
Blood Meal
Cherry Pitter
Collapsible Tomato Ladder
Fish Meal
Fly Traps
Grasshopper Spore
Lady Bugs
Praying Mantis
Repeating Mouse and Rat Traps
Steam Canner
Steam Juicer
Thuricide
Trichogramma Wasp

Black-seeded
Watermelon
(1/8 size)

Johnny's Selected Seeds
Foss Hill Road
P.O. Box 2580
Albion, ME 04910

Johnny's is a fairly young, quick-growing, respectable seed house. Seeds are untreated. A high percentage of the seed is actually grown by them organically. Seeds for colder, shorter seasons are emphasized. Professional, vigorous, top-quality approach to growing, testing and selling seeds. They offer select vegetables, beans, and grains (oats, wheat and dry corn) including some little known oriental vegetables.

VEGETABLES

Beans
 Champagne Bush Snap—62 days, up to 10 feet high
 Dry Beans
  Adzuki
  Black Turtle
  Dark Red Kidney
  Light Red Kidney
  Maine Yellow Eye
  Mung
  Pinto
  Seafarer
  Soldier
  Trout (Jacob's Cattle)
 Fava
 Fordhook® Bush Lima—85 days
 Lon's Champion Green Shell—68 days,
  use as green, shell or dry bean
 Proulder Bush Green—50 days
 Soybeans, dry
  Altona—100 days, our favorite
  Fiskeby V—91 days, early,
   closer spacing
  Panther—120 days, black
  Wilkin—106 days
 Soybeans, green vegetable
  Butterbeans—90 days
  Envy—75 days
 Sungold Bush Wax—47 days
Beets
 Early Wonder Tall Top—48 days

Altringham Carrot (1/5 size)

 Formanova LD—56 days, cylindra type
 Lutz Green Leaf—60 days, storage beet

Burdock
 Takinogawa Long

Cabbage Family
 Amager Green Storage Cabbage—
  120 days, for long-term storage
 Blue Danish Kohlrabi
 Brussels Sprouts
  Early Dwarf Danish—95 days, good variety
 Dominant Cauliflower—74 days, large solid heads
 Golden ·Acre Cabbage—58 days, early
 Harvester Kale—heavy frost tolerant
 Konserva Kale—heavy yields
 Late Danish L.D. Cabbage—105 days, storage type
 Matsushina Summer Sown Cabbage—85 days
 Nozaki Early Chinese Cabbage—60 days
 Vates Collards—tasty variety
 Waltham 29 Broccoli—92 days, autumn grower

Carrots
 Chantenay Advance—7-8 inches
 Scarlet Keeper—85 days, for storage
 Scarlet Nantes—good juicer

Corn, dry
 Longfellow Flint—yellow kernels
 Mandan Bride—white kernels

Corn, sweet
 Ashworth—69 days, yellow
 Bantam Evergreen—90 days, yellow
 Black Mexican
 Golden Bantam—83 days
 Golden Midget—75 days
 Midnight Snack

Popcorn
 Popwhite—for the North
 Rhodes Yellow Pop

*Long White Vertus, or
Jersey Navet, Turnip
(1/5 size)*

Cucumbers
 Lemon
 Marketmore 76—63 days, stays healthy during cool nights
 Mirella—Middle Eastern variety, short plump
 Northern Pickling—48 days, very early
 Spacemaster—dwarf plants, also good for patio boxes
 Suyolong Pickling

Eggplants
 Early Black—65 days

Greens
Edible Chrysanthemum
Shungiku
Escarole
Full Heart Batavian
Mustard
Green Wave
Parsley
Delikart Original—
71 days, Danish, early
Herbs
Garlic
German Chamomile
German Winter Thyme
Sorrel
Watercress
Many others
Jerusalem Artichokes
Stampede—extra early
Lettuce
Great Lakes "B" strain Head—77 days, heat tolerant
Ithaca M1 Head—60 days, early
Kagran Summer Bibb—54 days, very bolt resistant
King Crown Head—64 days
Romaine
Cosmo MC
Winter Density
Melons
Honey Gold No. 9 Japanese Watermelon—88 days, white flesh,
very small
Nuname Early Pickling—65 days
Sakata's Sweet Japanese Watermelon—88 days, 10-12 oz.
green flesh, skin changes color when ripe
Sweet Granite Cantaloupe—75 days, early
Onions
Downing Yellow Globe—105 days, hard storage variety
Leeks
King Richard L.D.—75 days
Stuttgarter Riesen Onion Sets—yellow storage variety
Peas
Oregon Sugar Edible Pod—62 days, good flavor
Showbiz Edible Pod Pole—70 days, tasty
Sparkle Bush Green—55 days, early, 18 inches high
Sugar Snap Pole—72 days
Wando Bush Green—70 days, heat tolerant

continued

*Flat Corsican Gourd
(1/12 size)*

Peas continued

Peas, soup
> Alaska Green—80 days, 30 inches high, for split peas
> Century Yellow—87 days, 4 feet high

Peppers
> Early Jalepeno Hot—68 days
> Karlo Romanian Yellow Hot—55 days
> Staddon's Select Sweet Bell—64 days

Salsify
> Gigantia Black

Squash
> Baby Blue Winter—95 days
> Bennings Green Tint Patty Pan—54 days, good flavor
> Bush Table Queen Winter—95 days
> Gold Nugget Bush Winter—85 days
> Red Kuri Winter—92 days
> Spaghetti Squash

Tomatoes
> Coldset—70 days
> Moira—76 days, bush beefsteak type
> Royal Chico Pear (Paste)—83 days
> Sub-Arctic—try spacing on
>> 15-inch centers
>>> S.A. Early—53 days
>>> S.A. Maxi—61 days
>>> S.A. Midi—56 days
>>> S.A. Plenty—59 days

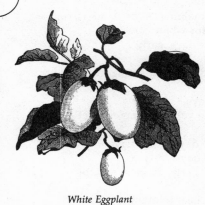

Eggplant

Eggplant needs a long hot summer to develop properly. The thin Japanese types grow better in slightly cooler areas. The small white eggplants are especially fun to grow. Seedlings should be spaced on 18-inch centers. Yields of 11-16 pounds are possible from 10 square feet. Once you learn how to use it, eggplant is amazingly versatile.

White Eggplant
(1/5 size)

• TIPS FROM THE TOP OF THE WORLD •

The Seed Finder

Turnips and Rutabagas
    Laurentian Rutabaga—95 days
    Ohno Scarlet Turnip—55 days

FRUITS

Strawberry
    Baron Solemacher Alpine—perennial bush

GRAINS

Alfalfa
    Iroquois
Buckwheat
Clover
    Mammoth Red
    Mixed White and Yellow Sweet
    White Dutch
Grain Amaranth
Millet
    Dawn Proso
Oats
Rapeseed
Sunflower
    Peredovik Russian—black, good for oil and eating
    Sundak—early
Wheat
    Pennal Soft Red Winter
    Polk Hard Red Spring
Winter Rye

*Long Yellow Capsicum
(1/3 size)*

TOOLS AND SUPPLIES

Bacillus Thuringiensis
Broadcast Seeders
Corn Sheller
Corona Burr Grain Mill
La Motte Soil Test Kits
Legume Inoculants
Maximum/Minimum Dial Thermometer
Rain Gauge
Soil Thermometer

*Chili Pepper,
or Chillies
(1/8 size)*

Common Garlic (1/4 size)

Garlic

Garlic is easy to grow but takes a long time to mature. Bulbs can be planted early in spring but fall plantings are best. Separate cloves and plant larger ones in a flat. When sprouted transplant onto 3- to 4- inch centers with the pointed ends barely emerging from the soil. They will stay in the ground through winter and spring and be harvested after the summer heat. Garlic "bulbs up" during the last 45 days of growth so be careful not to pull up too soon. Elephant Garlic is truly gargantuan but never gets that true garlic flavor and bite. For flavor and yield, red garlic (white cloves covered by reddish skins) is best. From 10 square feet the yield can be 12-24 pounds, worth $24-50.

• TIPS FROM THE TOP OF THE WORLD •

*Compact Bush Basil
Detached Branch
(scale not shown)*

Meadowbrook Herbs and Things
Whispering Pines Road
Wyoming, RI 02898   catalog $1

Meadowbrook specializes in herbs. All their seeds and dried herbs are bio-dynamically grown.

HERB SEEDS

Anise
Basil—2 kinds
Borage
Burdock
Caraway
Catnip
Chamomile—2 kinds
Chervil
Chives
Coriander
Cumin
Dill—2 kinds
Fennel—2 kinds
Feverfew
Flax—2 kinds
Foenogreek
Foxglove
Garden Cress
Garlic Chives
Horehound
Hyssop
Lamb's Ear
Lavender—2 kinds
Lemonbalm
Lovage

Mugwort
Mullein
Nettle
Oregano
Parsley—3 kinds
Pennyroyal
Peppermint
Red Valerian
Rosemary
Russian Tarragon
Sage—2 kinds
Savory—2 kinds
Soapwort
Sorrel—2 kinds
Spearmint
Sweet Marjoram
Thistle
    Holy
    Scotch
Thyme—2 kinds
Wormwood
Yarrow
    Red
    White
    Yellow

OTHER PRODUCTS

Animal Herb Blend
Cosmetics
Dried Herbs
Elixirs
Essential Oils
Herbal Teas
Many good books
Spices
Toiletries including Plant Toothpaste
   and Herbal Soaps

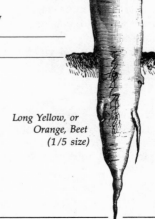

Long Yellow, or
Orange, Beet
(1/5 size)

Nourse Farms, Inc.
P.O. Box 485
RFD South Deerfield, MA 01373

Nourse Farms is a strawberry nursery. They also offer raspberry plants, asparagus and rhubarb. Stock is grown by them. Prices are good, though plants must be ordered in groups of 25 of each variety. All varieties are tested for the Northeast. Catalog descriptions are very detailed as to fruit size, flavor, keeping qualities, yields and disease resistance.

STRAWBERRIES

Bounty—late, Canadian, good flavor
Canoga—mid-season, produces large runner plants
Catskill—mid-season, 50-year-old variety
Darrow—early, good quality, flavor and yield
Earlidawn—early, frost resistant
Earliglow—early
Fairfax—excellent flavor but low yields
Fletcher—mid-season
Garnet—mid-season, good yields
Guardian—mid-season
Holiday—early mid-season, aromatic
Honeoye—early mid-season, good yields, winter hardy
Midland—early
Midway—mid-season, good yields, good shipper
Quinalt—everbearing, large, good quality
Raritan—early mid-season
Red Chief—good yields, sub-acid, mid-season
Red Coat—early, Canadian variety, winter hardy
Robinson—mid-season
Sparkle—late mid-season
Surecrop—mid-season
Sunrise—early
Vesper—late, good yields

RASPBERRIES

Brandywine—purple, winter hardy, summer
Heritage—red, everbearing, heavy fall crop
Reville—red, early, winter hardy, good yields
Taylor—red, mid-season, good yields

Early Flat Bassano
Beet
(1/5 size)

George W. Park Seed Co.
P.O. Box 31
Greenwood, SC 29647

Park is best known for one of the most complete flower seed catalogs, including many flowers usually started by professionals. They also sell equipment for hobbyists. They publish a gorgeous full-color catalog that includes an extensive selection of vegetables, herbs and ornamentals. We find their book *Park's Success With Seeds* to be very useful.

VEGETABLES

Dwarf Dutch, or Dwarf Crooked, Sugar Pea (1/10 size)

Artichokes
    Green Globe
    Jerusalem
Asparagus
    Paradise — very rust resistant
Beans
    Dried
            Garbanzo — Chick Pea
    Lima
            Bridgeton Bush — 65 days, early
            Dixie Butterpea — 75 days, meaty, delicious
            Jackson Wonder Bush — 65 days, speckled bean
            Large Speckled Christmas Pole — 88 days
            Speckled Dixie Butterpea — 75 days
    Snap
            Avalanche Bush — 57 days
            Contender Bush — 49 days, stress tolerant
            Goldcrop Bush Wax — 65 days
            Mountaineer White Half Runner Bush — 57 days
          ★ Remus Bush — 40 days, productive, easy to harvest
            Royal Burgundy Bush — 51 days
            Selma Star Pole — 60 days, productive
            Selma Zebra Pole — early, 6 feet high, tasty, light green
                with purple stripes
Beets
    Burpee's Golden — 55 days
    Cylindra — 60 days
    Green Top Bunching — 55 days, especially for tops
Cabbage Family
    Broccoli — Green Sprouting, multiple headed
    Cabbage
            All Seasons Wisconsin — 85 days

continued

 Mammoth Red Rock — 100 days, winter storer
 Michili Chinese
 Morden Dwarf — 55 days
Cauliflower
 Royal Purple — 95 days
 Snowball Self-Blanching — 70 days
Collards
 ★ Vates Non-heading — 75 days, winter hardy
Kale
 Dwarf Blue Curled Scotch Vates — 70 days
Kohlrabi
 Azur Star Purple — 50 days
Carrots
 Amstel — gourmet, 4 inches long
 Tendersweet — 75 days
Celeriac
 Large Smooth Prague — 110 days
Celery
 Giant Pascal — 120 days
 Heung Kunn Chinese

Siphon Gourd
(1/12 size)

Gourds

Recently some friends showed us their gourd collection. We were immediately taken by the beautiful and functional pitchers, sieves, vases, bowls and birdhouses they made. We would also like to try musical instruments/shakers and even a "thumb piano." Gourds are grown just like squash. Give them plenty of sun and lots of space. When soft they can be gently shaped to the form desired. Try 4-foot centers for spacing. For seeds and a good booklet on how to grow, shape, cure and use gourds, send $3.25 to Gourdjus, 556-61st St., Oakland, CA 94609.

Corn
    Golden Midget—30 inches high
    Trucker's Favorite White Open-Pollinated Sweet—65 days,
        good yields, keeps well
Cucumbers
    Tiny Dill—55 days
    ★Whopper Bush

Eggplant
    Morden Midget—65 days
Garlic
    Giant French Mild Elephant
Greens
    Comfrey
    Corn Salad—Broadleafed
    Curled Cress
    Dandelion
    Endive
        Green Curled Ruffed—95 days
    Mustard
        Southern Giant Curled—50 days
    Parsley
        Paramount—very dark green, very curled
    Rocket
    Sorrel
        Large Leaved French
    Watercress—True

Herbs
    Ambrosia
    Angelica
    Anise
    Basil
        Dark Opal
        Holy
        Italian
        Lemon
        Lettuce Leaf
        ★Picollo
    Borage
    Caraway
        Russian
    Catmint
    Catnip
    Chamomile
    Chervil
    Chia

*Seed-vessels of
Chili Pepper
(1/3 size)*

*Yellow Tankard
Mangold
(1/5 size)*

Chicory
  Large Rooted Madgeburg
Chinese (Garlic) Chives
Chives
Coriander
Cumin
Dill
Dwarf Bouquet Dill
Ginseng
Horehound
Hyssop
Lovage
Marjoram
Mint
  Curled Mint
  Lemon Balm
  Lemon Mint
  Pennyroyal
  Peppermint
  Spearmint
Mustard
  Black and Yellow
Oregano
Rosemary
Rue
Sage
Salad Burnet
Santolina
Savory
Sweet Fennel
Sweet Woodruff
Tansy
Tarragon
  Russian
Thyme
  Creeping
  Dwarf Compact Winter
  English
  Winter
Wormwood

Orange Jelly Turnip
(1/5 size)

Melons
  Cantaloupe
    ★Busheloupe
    Minnesota Midget—60 days
    Short 'n Sweet—75 days
  Honeydew
    ★Oliver Pearl Cluster Bush

Watermelon
    Golden Midget—65 days, green skin until ripe, then yellow
        with red flesh
    ★ Kengarden "Bush"
Mushroom
    Black Forest Kit
Okra
    Clemson Spineless—55 days
    Lee—50 days, early, "dwarf"
    Parks Candelabra Branching—about 55 days
    Red
    Spineless Green Velvet—58 days
Onions
    Crystal Wax—95 days, early white
    Ebenezer—105 days, yellow, stores well
    Leek—American flag, 130 days
    Red Hamburger—100 days
Peanuts
    Early Bunch Virginia—120 days
    Park's Whopper
    Spanish
    Valencia Tennessee Red—120 days
Peas
    Cowpeas
        Big Boy
        Dwarf California Blackeye—early
        Magnolia Blackeye
        Mississippi Purple
        Mississippi Silver—brown crowder type
        Purple Hull—crowder type
        White Lady
    Knight Dwarf—61 days, early, good yield
    Mighty Midget Dwarf—60 days, 6 inches high
    Patriot Bush—65 days, tasty, early
    Sugar Bon Bush Sugar Snap—about 59 days
    Sugar Snap Pole
Peppers
    Aconcagua Sweet—70 days
    Banana Sweet—65 days
    California Wonder Sweet—75 days
    Cherry Sweet—78 days
    Dutch Treat Sweet—70 days
    Large Red Thick Cayenne Hot—75 days
    Park's Dwarf Tequila Sunrise—golden orange
    Select Pimento Sweet—75 days
    Serrano Chili—for tabasco sauce
    Yolo Wonder Sweet—78 days

*Round Parsnip
(1/5 size)*

*Black-skinned
Sugar Beet
(scale not
shown)*

Potatoes
    Burbank Russet — 120 days
    Red McClure — 90 days
Potatoes, sweet
    All Gold — fast maturing
    Centennial — good yielder
    New Jewel — stores well
    Vineless Puerto Rico — "bush" type
Radishes
    Pax — 28 days, vigorous, white thick icicle type
Squash
    Pumpkin
        Big Moon — 110 days, up to 200 pounds
        Lady Godiva — 110 days, hull-less seeds
    Summer
        Bush Dark Green Zucchini — 50 days
        Seneca Gourmet — 46 days
        Vegetable Marrow — 60 days
    Winter
        Blue Hubbard — 115 days, stores well
        Improved Green Hubbard — stores well
        Show King — up to 400 pounds
        Waltham Butternut — good yields, stores well
Tomatoes
    ★ Burgess Early Salad — 45 days
    ★ Climbing Trip-L-Crop — 80 days, up to 8 feet, up to 3 bushels
        per plant
    Jubilee — good yields, orange flesh
    Manalucie — 85 days, very wilt and disease resistant
    Marglobe Supreme F — 73 days
    Rutger's California Supreme — 73 days
    Sugar Lump — for containers

*White
Carrot-shaped
Turnip
(1/5 size)*

USEFUL PLANTS

Chrysanthemum Cinerariifolium — source of Pyrethrum
Gourds — 25 selections, including:

Bottle	Orange
Dipper	Penguin
Dolphin	Snake
Luffa Sponge	Spoon
Miniature Bottle	Striped Pear

Ground Cos Lettuce (1/6 size)

Guayule—a natural rubber source
Hops
Jojoba
Safflower
Sesame
Tea

FRUITS

Blackberries
    Black Satin Thornless
    Darrow
Currant
    Red Lake
Elderberries
    Nova
    York
Fig
    Brown Turkey—everbearing, for tubs
Gooseberry
    Pixwell
Grapes
    Concord Seedless—purple, mid-season
    Lakemont Seedless—golden, hardy
    Muscadine Cowart—blue, productive
Pomegranate
    Wonderful
Raspberries
    Allen—black, good yield
    Fallgold—everbearing
    Heritage—red, everbearing
    Southland—red, two crops
Strawberries
    Plants
        Big Red—very early, June bearing
        Guardian
        Quinault
        Sequoia
        Sunburst
    Seeds
        Alexandria
        Alpine Yellow Fruited—birds do not eat!
        Baron Solemacher
        Rugen Improved
        Tuttifrutti

*Early Étampes
Cabbage
(1/12 size)*

continued

Florence, or
Magnum Bonum,
Cos Lettuce
(1/6 size)

Lettuce

Leaf lettuce and loosehead types such as Romaine, Prizehead and Bibb, are better nutritionally than head lettuce. The deeper the green, the higher the nutritional value. Some leaf varieties are especially beautiful and outer leaves can be harvested for continuous salads. Leaf lettuce seedlings are spaced on 8-inch centers and yield 20-40 pounds from 10 square feet. Heading and Loosehead lettuce varieties are transplanted on 12-inch centers and yield 15-30 pounds from 10 square feet. For best flavor and least bitterness, harvest early in the morning, around sunrise.

•— TIPS FROM THE TOP OF THE WORLD —•

FLOWERS

Achillea
    Yarrow—white, gold, red and pink
Aconitum
    Monkshood—2 selections
Ageratum
    Blue and White Mix
    Golden
Alstroemeria
    Lily of Peru—2 selections
Alyssum—all colors
    Snowcloth Improved
Amaranthus—4 selections
Amazon Lily

Saint-Laud Market-Garden
Melon
(1/5 size)

Anchusa—2 selections
Anemones—seeds or bulbs
Aquilegia-Columbine
    Dwarf
        Biedermeier
        Fairyland
        Flabellata Mini Star
    Maxi Star
    McKana Giant
    Olympia Red and Gold
    Park's Long Spurred Champion
    Rocky Mountain
    Teicheriana

Red-seeded Watermelon
(1/8 size)

Arctotis
    African Daisy
Asters—all kinds
    Massagno Cactus Mixed
    ★Powderpuff Super Bouquet Medium Tall Mix
Aubrieta
Balsam
Baptisia
Begonias—58 selections, seeds and bulbs;
   double ruffled in apricot, pink, yellow, scarlet and white
Belamcanda
    Blackberry Lily
Bletilla
    Hardy Chinese Orchid
Browallia
Bulbs
    Amaryllis—33 selections
    Caladiums—27 selections
        Dwarf Rosalie
        White Queen
    Cannas—16 selections
    Dahlias—37 selections, both seeds and bulbs
        Duet—beautiful deep red with white tips
        Sherwood Peach

Milan Purple-top
Strap-leaved
Turnip
(scale not shown)

    Freesias
    Gladiolas—27 selections
        Black Stallion—black red
        Sacred Heart—white with burgundy center and yellow eye
        Spectacular—golden yellow with some rose
        Sunburst Spire—dark and light orange with yellow
        Westminster Abbey—yellow with red throat
    Iris
        Kaempferi—Japanese

Ismene
    Peruvian Daffodil
Lilies—all kinds, seeds and bulbs
    Candy Lilies
    Daylily
    Gloriosa Lily
    Hedychium
        Ginger Lily
    Lily of the Valley
    Lycoris
        Spider Lily
    Waterlily
    Zephyranthes
        Fairy Lily
Montbretia
Oxalis—white, rose and lilac
Ranunculus—8 selections
Tigridia
    Mexican Shellflower
Tuberose—richly scented
Cabbage
    Flowering
Campanula
Candytuft
Carnations—19 selections
    All Season Blend
    Mixed Chabaud
    Mixed Fragrance—12 inches high
  ★ Orange Sherbet Chabaud
Celosia—all kinds
    Apricot Brandy
Cheiranthus
    Wallflower
Chrysanthemums—wonderful selection of seeds
Cineraria
Cleome
    Spider Flower
Coleus—16 selections
Coreopsis
    Dwarf Sunray—golden yellow
Cornflower
    Bachelor's Buttons
Cosmos—white, pink, crimson, orange-scarlet, yellow, golden
Cupid's Dart
★ Cyclamen—10 selections

Colorful Helena Mixture	Sweet Scented Mixture
Mixed Hardy	Victoria

Yellow Purple-top
Swedish Turnip
(1/5 size)

Delphinium—21 selections including Giants and Dwarfs
     Connecticut Yankees—blue, white, purple, lavender
Dianthus—Annual and Perennial, 14 selections
     Lace Mixture
     Mixed Sonnet—salmon, rose, red, white, lilac, pink
Dicentra
     Bleeding Heart
Digitalis
     Foxglove
Dimorphotheca
     ★African Daisy—beautiful sun-loving
Dodecatheon
     Shooting Star
Doronicum
     Leopard's Bane
Echinacea
     Coneflower—8-inch lavender-pink daisy-like flowers
Eremurus
     Foxtail Lady
Erythronium
     Dog's Tooth Violet
Euphorbia Polychroma—easy care perennial, masses of yellow flowers
Gaillardia
Gazania
Geraniums—41 selections
     Scented Geraniums
         Apple
         Bode's Peppermint
         Coconut
         Dr. Livingston—lemon
         Fair Ellen—Eucalyptus
         Oak Leaf
Gerbera
     Transuaal Daisy
Gypsophila
Heuchera
     Coral Bells
Hibiscus—4 selections
Hollyhock—5 selections
     Majorette—dwarf with full color range
     ★ Powderpuff—bushy 4-5 feet high
Hunnemannia
     Mexican Tulip Poppy
Hypericum
     St. John's Wort
Impatiens—68 selections including Tangeglow, a glowing orange

Early Dwarf
Red Tomato
(1/10 size)

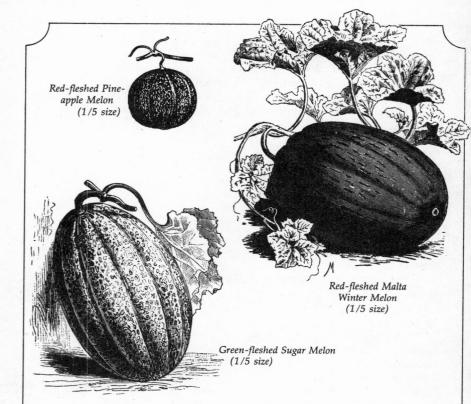

*Red-fleshed Pine-
apple Melon
(1/5 size)*

*Red-fleshed Malta
Winter Melon
(1/5 size)*

*Green-fleshed Sugar Melon
(1/5 size)*

Melons

Juicy, tasty melons from the garden are highly prized (along with strawberries). Cantaloupes without "netting" on the outsides are important for raised-bed gardening. The smooth skins are less likely to rot from the extra mini-climate moisture. Haogen (green-fleshed) from Burpee and Cantalun (orange-fleshed) from Vilmorin are good choices though Vilmorin seeds are very difficult to obtain unless you have a friend in France. Henry Field carries some interesting varieties. Our favorite Watermelon is the small, 3-pound Sugar Baby because it grows well in shorter, cooler growing seasons. Another good choice is the New Hampshire Midget—1 pound each, just enough for one person to eat. N.H. Midget Watermelons are planted on 12-inch centers. Cantaloupes, honeydews, and small watermelons go 15 inches apart. Larger watermelons go 18, 21 or 24 inches apart depending on size. Cantaloupe and Honeydew yields range from 7-14 pounds from 10 square feet and watermelon yields 10-32 pounds. Warm nighttime temperatures (60°F in the soil) are important to the setting of fruit.

Flowers continued

Kale
  Flowering
Lantana
Larkspur
Liatris
  Blazing Stars
Lobelia—6 selections
Lupines—12 selections, yellow, white, pink, red and blue-white
Machaeranthera
  Tahoka Daisy
Marigolds—62 selections
  Dwarf Double Crested
  Dwarf Janie
  Park's Nemagold—for nematode control
Mignonette—sweet-scented
Monarda
  Bee Balm
Morning Glory
  Cheerio—Scarlet
  Early Call Rose
  Improved Heavenly Blue
Myosotis
  Forget-Me-Not
Nasturtium
  Basket types—3 selections
  Climbing—2 types
  Dwarf—2 selections
Nicotiana
  Flowering Tobacco
Nierembergia
  Butterfly Flower
Pansies—20 selections
Penstemon
  Hyacinth Flowered Mixture
Petunias—55 selections
  Plum Pudding—blue, deep red, wine, pink, plum and yellow
Phlox
Platycodon
  Chinese Bellflower
Polemonium
  Jacob's Ladder
Poppies
  California   Oriental
  Iceland   Shirley

Early Russian Gherkin (1/8 size;
detached fruit, 1/5 size)

Portulaca
    Afternoon Delight
Primulas
    Primroses — 19 selections
Pyrethrum — 2 beautiful flowering Perennial types
Roses
    Miniatures — 13 colors
Rudbeckia
    Gloriosa Daisy
Salpiglossis
Salvia
    Flowering Sage — 16 selections including scarlet, orange, purple,
        white, blue and rose
Scabiosa
    Park's Giant Imperial Mixed
Schizanthus
    Butterfly Flower
Shasta Daisy
★ Snapdragons — 24 selections including dwarf varieties; red, white,
    scarlet, golden, lemon, crimson, bronze and pink
Stock
    ★ Trysomic 7-Week Blend — white, pink, rose, crimson, dark blue
        and purple
Strawflowers and Everlastings — great selection
    Money Plant
    Nigella
    Physalis
        Chinese Lantern
    Statice — 20 selections in lavender, white, blue, rose, yellow
        and golden
    Wood Rose
    and many others
Sunflowers
    Dwarf Sungold
    Giganteus
    Italian White
    Piccolo
★ Sweet Peas — 5 selections including dwarf
    and heat resistant types
Torenia
Tritoma
    Red Hot Poker
Trollius
Veronica
Viola
    Johnny Jump-Up

Common Bottle Gourd
(1/12 size)

Zinnias—61 selections
    Old Mexico
    Paint Brush
    Ruffles Mixed
    Small World—Deep cherry
Flowering Vines
    Asarina
    Cathedral Bells
    Chilean Jasmine
    Clematis—outstanding collection of these spectacular flowers
    Coral Vine
    Dutchman's Pipe
    Kudzu
    Madeira
    Mixed Lathyrus Latifolius
    Moon Vine
    Passion Vine
    Thunbergia
        Susie and White Wings
    Wisteria
    Yellow Jasmine
Mixtures
    California Flower Garden
    Cut Flower
    Fragrant
    Rock Garden Annuals
    Rock Garden Perennials
Wildflowers
    Central U.S. Mix
    Damp Places Mix
    Eastern U.S. Mix
    Northeastern U.S. Mix
    Prairie Grasses and Wildflowers Mix
    Rare Wildflowers—seeds for 29 annuals and 56 perennials
    Shady Mix
    Southeastern U.S. Mix
    Texas Mix
    Western U.S. Mix

White Stone, or Nonpareil,
Cabbage Lettuce
(1/6 size)

Early Flat Green Curled Savoy Cabbage
(1/12 size)

Common Welsh Onion, or Ciboule,
(1/8 size; detached stem,
1/4 size)

New Queen Onion
(1/3 size)

Italian Tripoli Onion ~
(1/5 size)

© 1982 1982 BY JOHN JEAVONS AND ROBIN LEEP

Onions

Onions are a staple in nearly every kitchen. For long storage try the Oregon Yellow Danvers from Abundant Life. For the highest yields try the elongated Red Torpedo onion. Transplant onions onto 3- to 4-inch centers. Yield is 20-40 pounds from 10 square feet. Torpedo onions yield 40-80 pounds from the same area.

• TIPS FROM THE TOP OF THE WORLD •

ORNAMENTALS AND HOUSE PLANTS

African Violets—beautiful selection
Cacti and Succulents

    Baby Toes   Mixed Rare Cactus
    Hardy Blend   Mixed Rare Succulents
    Hens and Chickens   Mixed South American
    Lithops (living stones) Ornamental Blend
    Mixed Mexican

Easter Eggplant
Ferns—15 selections
> Asparagus   Maidenhair
> Boston   Shade Growing—3 kinds

Flowering Grasses
> Animated Oats   Fountain Grass
> Bridal Veil   Grass Mixture
> Cloud Grass   Hare's Tail Grass
> Feather Grass   Quaking Grass

Goldfish Plant
Lawn Grass—9 selections including:
> ★Dense Shade Mix

Ornamental Peppers—7 selections
Rare Shrubs—from seed
> Azaleas   Rhododendron
> Camellia Japonica   Rosa Multiflora
> Chinese Dogwood   Snowball Bush
> Peony

Santolina—drought tolerant
Sensitive Plant

TOOLS, BOOKS AND GARDEN AIDS

Bean Tower—galvanized pole and nylon string
Books
> *Crockett's Indoor Garden*   *Park's Success With Bulbs*
> *Crockett's Victory Garden*   *Park's Success With Herbs*
> *Joy of Geraniums*   *Park's Success With Seeds*—very good

Hose Guides
"Lifetime" Markers
Pea Fence—galvanized wire panels
Peanut Legume Aid
Rocket Nutcracker
Waterproof Pen

Vosges White Carrot
(1/5 size)

Redwood City Seed Co.
P.O. Box 361
Redwood City, CA 94064   catalog 50¢

This seed company specializes in non-hybrid vegetables. We use them for many of our seed orders. Craig Dremann, the proprietor, is dedicated to preserving and promoting all manner of old-time, native, wild and/or nearly forgotten but useful plants. Here you will find the wild precursors of our lettuce, carrots and corn as well as old-time tomatoes, many oriental vegetables and a variety of excellent pamphlets from a variety of stores. Seeds come in no-frills packaging, prices are very reasonable, and the service reminds one of an old-time seed house.

VEGETABLES

Amaranth
    Joseph's Coat—bi-color for greens
    Ramdana—for high protein seed
Artichoke
    Globe
Beans
    Adzuki
    Asparagus
    Early Hakucho Soybeans—for cool climates
    Late Giant Black—seeded soybean
    Light-brown Tepary—drought and heat resistant
    Scarlet Runner
Burdock
    Edible
Cabbage Family
    Chinese Broccoli
    Georgia Collards
    Oriental Heading Cabbage—5 kinds
    Oriental Loosehead Cabbage—5 kinds
    Sea Kale Cabbage
    Snowpeak Tropical Cauliflower—summer growing, small heads
    Tall (Tree) Kale—up to 6 feet high
Cardoon
Carrots
    Carentan—4 inches long, coreless
    Japanese Long—130 days, up to 24 inches long, summer growing
    Kintoki—10 inches long, summer growing
    Senko—120 days, up to 20 inches long
    St. Valery—up to 10 inches, stores well
Celeriac

Dwarf Red Beet
(1/5 size)

Celery
        Tall Golden Self-blanching
Chicory
Corn
        Adams Extra Early Tortilla Corn—65 days
        Black Mexican Sweet Corn
        Golden Midget Yellow—30-36 inches tall
        Golden Popcorn
        Golden Sunshine Yellow—8-inch long ears
        Hickory King Tortilla Corn
        Stowell's Evergreen White—grown since 1860, 14-18 rows
            of kernels
        Strawberry Popcorn
        Teosinte—Mexican ancestor of corn
        White Hull-less Popcorn
Cucumbers
        Aodai Japanese Climbing   National Pickling
        Armenian   Soo-yoh—no bitterness
        Heiwa Green Prolific   West Indian Gherkin
        Lemon
Eggplant
        Chinese Long
        Florida High Bush
        White—resembles a hen's egg

Garlic set
Greens
        Comfrey
        Corn Salad
        Garden Cress
        Green Curled Endive
        Hamburg Turnip Rooted Parsley

*Early Purple-top
Munich Turnip
(1/5 size)*

        Japanese Greens—6 varieties
        Miner's Lettuce—very tasty, found wild in woodlands
        Munsterlander Spinach—heat and frost tolerant
        Mustard
                Florida Broadleaf
                Nan Foon Non-heading—50 days
                Osaka Purple Leaved—80 days or 150 days in winter
                South China Heading
        Mustard Spinach—will grow year-round
        New Zealand Spinach—drought resistant
        Orach
        Rhubarb Red
        Rocket Salad
        Sohshu Spinash—40 days, smooth leaved, fast growing
        Sorrel—3 kinds
        Watercress

Herbs
- Aloe Vera
- Anise
- Basil
    - Bush
    - Lettuce-leaved
- Betony
- Borage—blue flowers taste like sweet cucumbers and are colorful in salads
- Caraway
- Catnip
- Chamomile
    - German and Roman—both true type and a petal-less type for use in herbal lawns
- Chervil
- Chives and Garlic Chives
- Coriander (Cilantro)
- Creeping Thyme
- Cumin
- Dill
- Edible Dandelion
- Elecampane
- Fenugreek
- Garden Burnet
- Ginseng (American)
- Goldenseal
- Good King Henry—like spinach and asparagus
- Henbane
- Horehound
- Hyssop
- Leopard's-bane
- Marshmallow
- Mugwort
- Mullein
- Pennyroyal
- Shepherd's Purse
- Spearmint
- Summer Savory
- Tansy
- True Fennel
- Wormwood
- Yarrow

Leeks

Chinese Cabbage
(1/10 size)

Lettuce
  All Year-Round Semi-heading—summer growing
  Buttercrunch Butterhead
  Common Green Cutting
  Imperial Winter
  Prizehead—beautiful multi-colored
  Wild—2 varieties
Melons
  Banana Muskmelon
  Casaba
      Golden Beauty—120 days
  Crenshaw—100 days
  Golden Pear Giant Japanese
  Honeydew—115 days
  Kaho Chinese Watermelon—87 days, about 3 pounds
Onions
  Australian Brown—long storer
  Evergreen Bunching
  Italian Red Torpedo—extra long
  Shallots
  Southern White Globe—good storer
  Welsh—grown for tops as seasoning
      Kujyo Regular—overwinters
      Yakko Summer—heat tolerant
  White Creole Regular—good for drying
Peanuts
  Virginia
Peas
  Little Marvel
  Nippon Kinusaya Early Edible Podded Sugar
  Sierra Madre del Sur—for split pea soup
  Sugar Snap
Peppers
  Bull Nose Sweet Green
  Chilis

California	Pasilla
De Arbol	Pequin
De Comida	Red Chili
Jalepeno	Serrano
Mexican Negro—black	Tabiche
New Mexico	

  Long Narrow Red Cayenne
  Pepperoncini Hot
  Pimento
  Santaka—very hot!

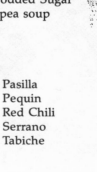

White Belgian Carrot
(1/5 size)

Radishes
    Chinese
    Japanese—Spring, Summer and Winter types including:
        Awa Pickling
        Sakurajima Mammoth—150 days, up to 1 foot diameter
            and 40-65 pounds
Rhubarb
    Queen Victoria
Salsify
    Mammoth Sandwich Island
Squash
    "Black" Zucchini—very dark green, vine
    Fultsu Early Black Pumpkin—yellow flesh
    Large White Manteca Pumpkin
    Naked Seeded Winter
    Sugar (New England Pie) Pumpkin
    Sweet Chestnut Red Winter—25 days after transplanting,
        very fast growing, 4-5 pounds
Tomatoes
    Early Large Red—an old-fashioned early
Turnips
    Shoigoin—for greens, 25 days, fast growing
    Snowball
    Superba Rutabaga

Double-curled Dwarf Parsley (1/5 size)

Parsley

Biointensively grown parsley is especially tasty and better than vitamin tablets for vitamin A and iron. Transplant seedlings onto 4-inch centers. Yield is 5-10 pounds from 10 square feet. Both curled and flat Italian types are good.

• TIPS FROM THE TOP OF THE WORLD •

USEFUL PLANTS

Black Seeded Sunflower—mainly for oil
Broom Corn
Carob
Coffee
Cotton
Dye Plants—8 listings
Flax
Honey Locust
Hops
Jojoba
Kudzu
Luffa Sponge
Sesame
Spanish Broom—basket and fiber plant
Tea

Water Chestnut (1/10 size)

FRUITS—FROM SEED

Blueberry
Buffalo Berry
Cranberry
Date
Elderberry
Garden Huckleberry
Jujube
Kiwi
Olive
Papaya—dwarf
Passion Fruit—up to 20-30 foot vines
Pineapple Guava
Pomegranate
Strawberry
      Baron Solemacher—everbearing

White Portugal Onion
(1/3 size)

NUTS

European Filbert
Live Oak
Pecan
Pine Nut—3 varieties

Dwarf Early Green Curled Savoy Cabbage
(1/12 size)

Parsnips

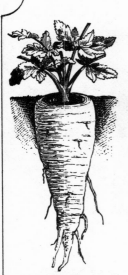

Parsnips and potatoes are good winter vegetables. In our area we can leave them in the ground over winter and harvest as needed for the table. Sprinkle wood ashes into the soil to protect from root maggots. Plant parsnips on 3-inch centers and harvest after frost. Yield is 23-48 pounds from 10 square feet.

Hollow Crown, or Student, Parsnip (1/5 size)

Long Parsnip (1/5 size)

• TIPS FROM THE TOP OF THE WORLD •

continued

FLOWERS

California Poppies
     Golden
     Mahogany—red
     Purple
     White
California Wildflower Mixes
Morning Glory
     Blue Star
     Flying Saucers
     Heavenly Blue
     Pearly Gates
     Scarlet O'Hara
Pyrethrum

Docteur Nicaise Strawberry

ORNAMENTALS

Sensitive Plant
Sequoia—2 varieties, Redwood Trees

The Seed Finder

BOOKS AND PAMPHLETS

Avocado Care in the Home Orchard
The Basils
Biological Control of Plant Pests
Planting Black Walnut for Timber
Carob Culture in California
Collecting and Handling Seeds of Wild Plants
Cranberry Culture
Developing Resistant Plants
Dyes and Dyeing
Dye Plants and Dyeing
Growing Pomegranates in California
Growing Seed Crops
Home Dyeing With Natural Dyes
Home Production of Olives
Hop Production
Jujube or 'Chinese' Date Cultivation
The Loquat
Papaya Culture in California
Pistachio Nut
Tea for Home Use
Teosinte
Tobacco: Cultivation and Curing
Tobacco: Methods of Curing
Tree Crops Catalog—particularly good! Costs $1.00.
Weeds Used in Medicine
Your Water Supply and Forests

Strasbourg Pear-shaped, Non
Plus Ultra, or Intermediate
Dark Beet (1/5 size)

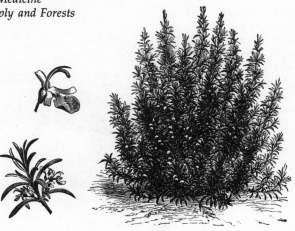

Rosemary (1/15 size; detached branch, 1/3 size;
detached flower, natural size)

Seed Savers Exchange
Kent Whealy
Rural Route 2
Princeton, MO 64673

This is a network of gardeners keeping heirloom vegetable strains alive. You send $2 for the yearbook which lists what members have available. It also lists Collectors, Commercial Seed Sources, includes a helpful Seed Saving Guide and other useful information. They are always looking for additional sources of old vegetable varieties.

We can hardly even give a sample of the listings—it will take all winter just to read through this one. Many are seeds grown by American Indians, brought from the Old Country or have been discovered and passed on in someone's family. Some of the ones that caught our eye:

Belieluck Yugoslavian Garlic
Black Prince Dwarf Hot Pepper
China Hot Pepper
Cliff Dweller Bean
Crimson Pod Cornfield Beans
Drought Resistant Okra
German Giant Tomato
Italian Sweet Potato
Logan Giant Pole Beans
Painted Lady Limas
Perennial Garlic
Peruvian Corn
Pomeranian Lettuce
Purple Guatemalan Broccoli
Purple Seeded Sweet Corn
Red Multiplier Onions
Red Tennessee Peanut
Tahitian Squash
Ukranian Giant
    Sunflower

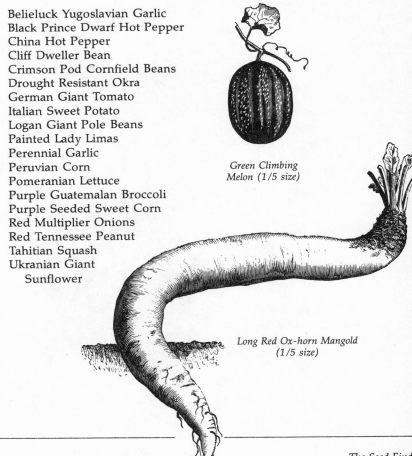

*Green Climbing
Melon (1/5 size)*

*Long Red Ox-horn Mangold
(1/5 size)*

R.H. Shumway
628 Cedar Street
P.O. Box 777
Rockford, IL 61105

Shumway offers a refined, well-organized and colorful catalog with a good selection of everything from vegetables to flowers to fruit and nut trees to berries. We use them mainly for cover crops that are often hard to find elsewhere.

VEGETABLES

Artichoke
    Large Green Globe
Beans
    Dry
            Dark Red Kidney
            Great Northern White
            Mung
            Pinto
            Wren's Egg—dwarf
    Lima
            Early Giant Bush
            Fordhook® Bush
            King of the Garden Pole—88 days
            Sievas Pole—78 days
    Snap
            Asparagus Green Pole
            Century Gold Wax Bush
            Giant Stringless Green Pod Bush
            Golden Wax Bush—50 days
            Half Runner White Bush
            Missouri Wonder Green Pole
            Purple Pod Bush
            Roma Bush
            Scarlet Runner Pole
            Speckled Cranberry Green Pole
            Tenderette Bush Green
            Topcrop Bush Green—49 days
Beets
    Burpee's Golden
    Cherry—early
    Cylindra
    Extra Early Egyptian—36 days

Common, or Plain,
Parsley
(1/5 size)

White Paris Cos
Lettuce
(1/6 size)

Cabbage Family
    Cabbage
        Autumn King Fall
        Chinese—73 days, up to 5 pounds
        Danish Ballhead Winter
        Dwarf Morden—for patio boxes
        Early Flat Dutch
        Premium Late Flat Dutch
        Ruby Ball Red—68 days
    Cauliflower
        Extra Early Snowball—50 days
    Kale
        Dwarf Blue Curled
        Dwarf Green Curled
        Tall Green Scotch Curled
Carrots
    Early Chantenay
    Royal Chantenay
    Tiny Sweet—3 inches long, for window boxes
Celeriac
Corn
    Calico Indian Ornamental
    Country Gentleman
    Golden Midget—for tub culture

detached fruit,
(1/5 size)

Prickly, or
West Indian,
Gherkin
(1/12 size)

Peanuts

A loose warm soil is especially important for peanuts. After flowering, umbilical cords shoot out and penetrate the soil where the peanuts are formed. Children especially like to harvest the plants, finding the peanuts entangled in roots underground. Transplant peanuts onto 9-inch centers. Yield is 10-20 pounds from 10 square feet. For areas with short growing seasons or cooler nights, try the Early Spanish No. 1 from Gurney.

Peanut (1/10 size;
detached fruit, 1/2 size)

• TIPS FROM THE TOP OF THE WORLD •

Improved Golden Bantam
Six Shooter Sugar—white kernels, up to 6 ears per plant
White Midget—for tub culture
Cucumbers
American Climbing—58 days
Everbearing—52 days
Longfellow
Midget—for patio boxes
Shumway's Fancy Pickling—50 days
Spacemaster Bush—60 days
Eggplant
Ichiban—61 days, early
Garlic
California White
Jumbo Elephant
Greens
Broad Leaf Escarole
Broadleaved Sorrel
Corn Salad
Mustard
Chinese Broad Leaf
Southern Curled
Parsley
Hamburg Rooted
Moss Curled
Salad King Endive
Spinach
Giant Thick Leaved
Indian Summer
New Zealand
Upland Cress
Watercress
Herbs
Borage
Chives
Hyssop—white, pink and blue (for honeybees)
Wormwood
Horseradish
New Bohemian
Lettuce
Bibb
Buttercrunch Butterhead—57 days
Dark Green Boston Butterhead
New York Special No. 12 Crisphead—up to 3 pounds
Tom Thumb—for tub culture

Orthe Carrot
(1/5 size)

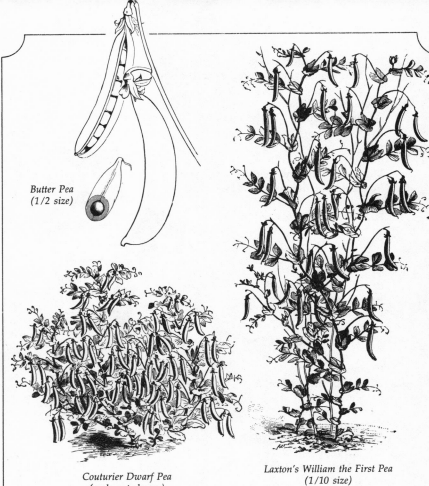

Butter Pea
(1/2 size)

Couturier Dwarf Pea
(scale not shown)

Laxton's William the First Pea
(1/10 size)

Peas

Bush or dwarf pea varieties yield almost as well as pole varieties with less work although pole peas are easier to harvest. For a treat try the Little Sweetie Edible Pod Pea from Stokes. Sugar Snap peas are also delicious. It is no wonder they are the hottest vegetable "discovery" of the past few years. Seeds are often in short supply. Once you have them growing save some seed for yourself and friends. Plant Bush Peas on 3-inch centers and Pole Peas on 4-inch centers. From 10 square feet the harvest will be about 5-10 pounds for regular peas in the pods, 5-10 pounds for sugar snap peas and 2½-5 pounds for sugar peas.

continued

Mangels
- Colossal Long Red
- Giant Half Rose Sugar Top
- Improved White Sugar Beet

Melons
- Banana
- Cantaloupe
    - Golden Champion—75 days, early and tasty
    - Honey Rock
    - Midget—for tub culture
    - Penn Sweet
    - Tip Top Shumway's Giant
- Watermelon
    - Black Diamond—up to 50 pounds
    - Citron Red-seeded—95 days, white flesh
    - Coles Early—75 days
    - Golden Midget—for tub culture
    - Ice Box—for tub culture

Mushroom Spawn and Mushroom "Farm"

Okra
- Clemson Spineless
- Dish Cloth
- Perkin's Mammoth Long Pod

Onions
- Ebenezer—light yellow, good storer
- Red Wethersfield Hamburger Onion

Peanut
- Improved Virginia—120 days

Very Early Paris Savoy Cabbage (1/12 size)

Peas
- Brown Crowder Mississippi Cowpeas—60 days, up to 2 crops in long season
- Early Frosty Green Bush—64 days
- Edible Pod Black Eye Cowpeas—60 days
- Little Marvel Green Bush—58 days, 15-18 inches high
- Sugar Snap Pole Green—Edible Pod
- Two Hundred Fold Green Bush—60 days, high yields, 22 inches high

Pepper
- California Wonder
- Chinese Giant
- Dutch Treat Sweet—68 days, 15-18 inch plants
- Golden California Wonder
- Jalapeno—Hot
- Long Slim Cayenne—Hot
- Mammoth Ruby King

Common, French, or Narrow-leaved Thyme (1/8 size; detached sprig, 1/2 size)

Peppers, Sweet

The green bell peppers are probably best known, though pimentos are gaining in popularity. Pimentos are the size and color of tomatoes with a crunch and flavor very similar to bell peppers. Bell peppers left on the plant will turn red when they mature, being sweeter and higher in vitamin C than in their green stage. There are many other shapes and colors from the long yellow banana pepper to the Sweet Chocolate Bell offered by Abundant Life. All the "sweet peppers" take more hot weather to mature than the hot or chili peppers. Sweet pepper seedlings are transplanted onto 12-inch centers when weather is warm. Yield is 8-13 pounds from 10 square feet.

*Large Bell Pepper
or Capsicum
(1/3 size)*

• TIPS FROM THE TOP OF THE WORLD •

continued
Potato
 New Golden Jewel Sweet Potato
Radish
 Sakurajima Winter—very large
 White Strasburg—large icicle type
Rhubarb
 Victoria
Squash
 Blue Hubbard—up to 15 pounds
 Jersey Golden Acorn
 New Buttercup
 New Waltham Butternut
 Pumpkin
  Mammoth Golden Cushaw
  Pot Iron or King—up to 100 pounds, for stock feed
 Vegetable Spaghetti

*Lebœuf Lettuce
(scale not shown)*

Tomatoes
    Abraham Lincoln   Pritchard's Scarlet Topper
    Jubilee—golden orange   Roma Pear
    Ponderosa—pink   Tiny Tim—for tub culture
Turnip
    Early Snowball—45 days

USEFUL PLANTS

Gourds
    Calabash
    Nest Egg
Kudzu
Luffa Sponge
Safflower

FRUITS

Apples
    Jonathan—standard or dwarf
    Red Delicious—standard or dwarf
    Winesap—standard
    Yellow Delicious—standard or dwarf
    Yellow Transparent—standard or dwarf
    5-in-1—the above 5 grafted onto 1 tree
    Dolga Crab
    McIntosh—standard or dwarf
Apricots
    Chinese Early Golden Dwarf
    Manchu
Blackberry
    New Darrow
Blueberries
    Bluecrop
    Jersey
    Top Hat—miniature for tub culture
Boysenberry
    New Thornless
Cherries
    Sour

Giant Rocca Onion
(1/3 size)

        Montmorency
        North Star—dwarf
    Sweet
        Bing   Kansas Sweet
        Black Tartarian   Royal Ann

Currants
    Red Lake
Elderberries
    Adams
    Johns
Gooseberries
    Pixwell
Grapes
    Buffalo
    Caco
    Concord
    Niagara
    Ontario
    Seedless
        Concord
        Interlaken
        Royal Blue
        Suffolk Red
Lemon
    Dwarf Everbearing
Nectarine, Nectarina, extra dwarf

*Dwarf Fan, or
Cluster, Bean
(pods 1/3 size)*

Peppers, Hot

Hot peppers are very popular here in California and we are glad to see seed companies increasing their selection. One person we know grows over 30 different kinds. Most are quite easy to dry for winter use. Just string them on a thread and hang in a warm place. Just one will turn the blandest soup into a winter warmer. The hottest ones are Serrano and Santaka. Cayenne peppers are transplanted onto 12-inch centers. Yield is 2.5 pounds from 10 square feet. Hot peppers are high in vitamins A and C and iron.

*Long Cayenne Pepper
(1/3 size)*

The Seed Finder

Orange
    Dwarf Everbearing—decorative
Peaches
    Belle of Georgia
    Early Elberta
    Elberta—also as dwarf
    Golden Glory—extra dwarf, only 4 feet
    Hale Haven—also as dwarf
    Red Haven—also as dwarf
Pears
    Bartlett—also as dwarf
    Bosc
    Clapp's Favorite—dwarf
Plums
    Burbank
    Shiro—golden yellow
    Stanley—also as dwarf
Raspberries
    Black
        Black Hawk
        Cumberland
        Jet
    Gold
        Forever Amber
    Heritage Red—2 crop
    Latham
    Mammoth Red Thornless
    New Fall Red Everbearing
Strawberries
    Chief Bemidji
    Ozark Beauty

Mosbach Winter
Kale
(scale not shown)

NUTS

Black Walnut
Butternut
Chinese Chestnut
Colby Pecan
English Walnut
Hall's Almond
Major Pecan

Round Purple
Eggplant
(1/4 size)

FLOWERS

Angel's Trumpet Datura
Apricot Brandy Dwarf Celosia Plumosa
Baby's Breath
Bee Balm
Begonias
Bird of Paradise
Bulbs
     Crocus
     Daffodils
     Hyacinths
     Narcissus
     Ranunculus
Burning Bush
Crimson "Woolflower" Celosia
Double Mixed
     Moss Rose Portulaca
Everlasting Sweet Pea
Giant White Shasta Daisies
Grandmother's Old Fashioned Garden—mix
Hibiscus
Ice Plant—succulent
Miniature Roses—yellow, pink and crimson
Moonflower Vine—blooms at night
Ornamental Grasses
Passion Flower
Patens Blue Salvia
Pink Heather Alyssum
Sensitive Plant
Snowball Feverfew—an insecticide
Spider Plant
St. John's Fire Salvia
Strawflowers
Summer Carnival Double Hollyhocks—scarlet, dark rose, pink, yellow, white
Trumpet Creeper—scarlet-orange flowers
and many other flowers

Docteur Morere Strawberry

GRAINS AND COVER CROPS

Available in small and large amounts.

Alfalfa—4 varieties
Alsike Clover

Birdsfoot Trefoil
Boone County White Seed Corn
Canadian Field Peas
Cowpeas
Crimson Clover
Fodder Cane
Forest City Shady Lawn Seed
Foxtail Millet
Hairy Winter Vetch
Hegari Sudan Grass
Hubam Sweet Clover
Japanese Buckwheat
Japanese (Duck) Millet
Ladino Clover
Longfellow Yellow Flint Seed Corn
Mammoth Red Clover
Mammoth Russian Sunflower
Medium Red Clover
Orchard Grass
Pasture Mixes
Penngift Crownvetch
Rapeseed
Shumway's Goliath Silo (Ensilage) Seed Corn
Sugar Drip Sorghum Cane
Sweet Sudan Grass
Timothy
Timothy and Alsike Mixture
White Dutch Clover
Yellow Blossom Sweet Clover

Borage
(1/8 size)

TOOLS AND SUPPLIES

Adjustable Vegetable Slicer
Apple Parer, Corer, Slicer
Berry Screen
Blood Meal
Bone Meal
Fish Emulsion
Flower Dri Kit
Food Preservation Supplies
Fruit Picker
Grape Spiral
Havahart Traps—4 sizes
Jelly Strainer
Kernel Kutter
Ladybugs

Green-fleshed Malta
Winter Melon
(1/5 size)

Liquid Seaweed
Neegards—protect knees when weeding
Nitragin Inoculants—7 kinds
Pea and Bean Sheller
Praying Mantis
Pressure Canner
Pumpkin Screen
Pyrethrum
Red Earthworms
Roll-A-Hose Guide—spins hoses easily around garden corners
1% Rotenone
Soil and Compost Sieve—with manual rotary blades
Thuricide—biological control of moths/caterpillars
Tree Tanglefoot
Victorio Strainer

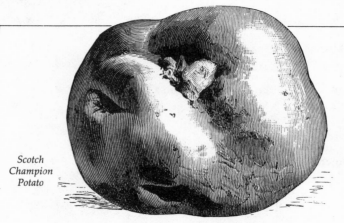

Scotch Champion Potato

Potatoes—"Irish"

If you grow nothing else, we highly recommend potatoes. They are easy to grow, harvesting them is like finding gold in your backyard and the flavor is way beyond any store-bought spuds. Potatoes originally came from Peru where they grow them in more colors than easter eggs. Simply cut potatoes into pieces the size of eggs (small ones can be planted whole) and place in the bed on 9-inch centers, 6-9 inches deep. Harvest about 4 months later when leaves have all completely died down. Ask the grocer if you use potatoes from the grocery to plant. Sometimes they are sprayed with growth retardant for a longer shelf life. We think red potatoes are especially rich tasting. White potatoes are drier and make better french fries or hash browns.

Potatoes yield 20-40 pounds from 10 square feet.

• TIPS FROM THE TOP OF THE WORLD •

Stark Brothers Nurseries
Louisiana, MO 63353

Stark Brothers is one of the oldest and best known mail order fruit tree houses. Nearly 100 years ago they received rights to the plant developments of Luther Burbank. Today they specialize in "Stark-spur" apples, trees with more fruiting spurs per limb and other Stark exclusive stock. Of course everything is described as "amazing," "luscious," "mouth-watering," and "vigorous," so it is best to check another reference. Our favorite fruit tree book is *Western Fruit, Berries and Nuts* (see Bibliography). Stark Brothers also offers many money-saving assortments. Check these out if you are planning a whole orchard.

VEGETABLES

A "no-nonsense" assortment of basic vegetable seeds is offered, including the latest All-America winners.

FRUITS

Apples
    Arkansas Black—standard, good keeper
    Cortland—standard, for cider, salads
    Grimes Golden—standard, tangy
    Idared—standard
    Jerseymac—standard and dwarf
    Lodi—standard, good for apple butter
    Ozard Gold—standard
    Prima—dwarf and standard
    Priscilla—dwarf and standard
    Sir Prize—standard

Early White-tipped
Scarlet Turnip Radish
(1/3 size)

    Stark®
        Blushing Golden—dwarf and standard, good keeper
        Earliest—dwarf and standard
        Gala—dwarf and standard
        Golden Delicious—standard
        Jon-A-Red—dwarf and standard
        Jonalicious—dwarf and standard
        Lodi—dwarf and standard
        Lura Red—standard
        McIntosh—standard
        Red Bouquet Delicious—dwarf
        Red Northern Spy—standard
        Red Rome Beauty—standard, for baking

> Red Winesap — standard
> Red York — standard
> Scarlet Staymared — standard, spicy winter variety
> Winesap — dwarf and semi-dwarf

Starking Full Red Delicious® — dwarf and standard
Starkrimson Red Delicious® — dwarf and semi-dwarf

Starkspur®

> Earliblaze — dwarf and semi-dwarf
> Golden Delicious — dwarf and semi-dwarf
> McIntosh — dwarf and semi-dwarf
> Red Gold — dwarf and semi-dwarf
> Red Rome Beauty — semi-dwarf

Tropical Beauty — dwarf and standard, grows in warmer climates

Apricots

> Hungarian Rose — standard, sweet
> Stark Giant Tiltson® — standard, large
> Stark's Earli-Orange® — semi-dwarf
> Wilson Delicious — semi-dwarf and standard, hardy,
>   heavy bearer

Berries

> Blackberry
>> Darrow
>> Thornfree
> Blueberries
>> Bluecrop
>> Corville
>> Earliblue
>> Elliot
> Boysenberry, thornless
> Currant
>> Red Lake
> Elderberries
>> Nova
>> York
> Gooseberry
>> Pixwell
> Rabbiteye Blueberries — for the South
>> Delite
>> Tifblue
> Raspberries
>> Black Hawk — black
>> Bristol — black
>> Fallgold — everbearing
>> Heritage Everbearing — red

Powder-horn Gourd
(1/12 size)

Latham—red
Southland—red
Strawberries
Midway—for the North
Ogallala—everbearing
Ozark Beauty—everbearing
Pocahontas—for the South
Stark Red Giant®
Sunrise—early
Sure Crop

Cherries
Bing—standard, red, sweet
Early Richmond—standard, red, sour, early
Emperor Francis—standard, reddish, sweet
Hedelfingen—standard, red, sweet
Meteor—dwarf, red, sour, hardy
Napoleon (Royal Ann)—standard, golden, sweet,
good for canning
North Star—dwarf, red, sour, hardy
Schmidt's Biggareau—standard, red, sweet
Stark Lambert®—red, sweet, hardy
Stark Montmorency®—standard
Starkgold®—standard, sweet, spicy
Starkspur Montmorency®—semi-dwarf, red, sour, for pies
Suda Hardy—dark red, sour, hardy, late ripening
Van—standard, red, sweet, hardy
Venus—standard, red, sweet
Vista—standard, red, sweet, early

Olive-shaped
Scarlet
Radish
(1/3 size)

Grapes
Buffalo—blue-black
Catawba—red
Concord—blue-black
Delaware—red
Golden Muscat
Himrod Seedless—light green
Interlaken Seedless—green
Lakemont—green seedless, good flavor
Niagara—greenish white
Stark Blue Boy®
Steuben—lavender
Suffolk Red Seedless
Vinered
Wine Grapes

French Breakfast
Radish (1/3 size)

Aurora—white	De Chaunak—red
Baco Noir—red	Foch—red
Cascade—red	Seyval Blanc—white

Potatoes, Sweet

Sweet potatoes are higher in calcium and calories than "Irish" potatoes. Many people eat the leaves which are also nutritious. Sweet potatoes need hot weather to grow. Plant whole sweet potatoes in flats until sprouted. Then nick off leaf/root combinations with a small amount of connecting potato. Transplant these starts 4-6 inches deep and 9 inches apart. Yield is 16-40 pounds from 10 square feet.

Red Sweet Potato (1/8 size)

• TIPS FROM THE TOP OF THE WORLD •

---

continued

Nectarines

    Golden Treasure—a natural miniature tree, 6 feet
    Mericrest—standard, hardy
    Stark Delicious®—standard, large
    Stark Earliblaze®—standard
    Stark Redgold®—standard
    Stark Sunglo®—standard, tasty

Peaches

    Babygold 5—standard, for canning
    Belle of Georgia—standard
    Burbank July Elberta®—dwarf and standard
    Candor—early canning variety
    Compact Redhaven—dwarf
    Cresthaven—standard
    Desertgold—grows in warmer climates
    Fantastic Elberta—standard
    Glohaven—standard
    J.H. Hale—standard
    Loring—standard
    Madison—good cropper, winter hardy
    Monroe—standard
    Redhaven—standard, hardy
    Redskin—standard
    Reliance—winter hardy freestone

Bishop's Early Dwarf Pea (1/10 size)

The Seed Finder

Peaches continued
  Stark®
    Autumn Gold—early fall-ripening freestone
    Earliglo—dwarf and standard
    Early Elberta—standard
    Early White Giant—dwarf and standard
    Elberta Queen—dwarf and standard, good canner
    Frostking—winter hardy
    Hal-Berta Giant—standard
    Honeydew Hale—standard, large freestone
    Sunbright—standard
    Sure-Crop—hardy white clingstone
  Starking Delicious®—dwarf and standard
  Sunapee—hardy
Pears
  Anjou—dwarf and standard
  Bartlett—dwarf and standard
  Buerre Bosc—standard, winter variety
  Comice—standard, good winter variety
  Duchess—dwarf and standard, large
  Fame—dwarf
  Kieffer—standard, winter
  Moonglow—dwarf and standard, early
  Seckel—dwarf and standard, "sugar" type
  Stark Jumbo Dwarf®
  Starking Delicious®—dwarf and standard
  Starkrimson®—dwarf, red skinned
  Tyson—dwarf and standard, early "sugar" type
Plums
  Blue (Prune) Plums
    Blufre—standard, delicious
    Burbank Grand Prize®—standard, large
    Earliblume—standard
    Stanley—standard, high yielding
  Burbank Elephant Heart®—standard, large
  Burbank Red Ace®—standard
  Cherry Plum
    Stark Giant®—standard
  Ember—standard
  Giant Damson—self-pollinating
  Green Gage—standard
  Ozark Premier—standard
  Redheart—semi-dwarf and standard
  Reine Claude Conducta—standard
  Santa Rosa—standard, originated by Luther Burbank

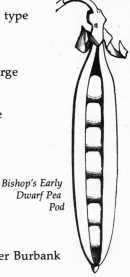

*Bishop's Early
Dwarf Pea
Pod*

continued

Spanish Gourd or Pumpkin (scale not shown)

Étampes Pumpkin (1/10 size)

Mammoth Pumpkin (1/10 size)

Pumpkins

Pumpkins are the most familiar form of winter squash, those squashes with a hard shell that can be stored over winter but must be grown during hot summer months. "Pumpkin" pie can be made from a variety of winter squashes including butternut and acorn. Transplant seedlings of smaller pumpkins onto 18-inch centers, medium ones 24 inches apart, and large ones 30 inches apart. Yields are 10-20 pounds from 10 square feet. Don't forget to toast and eat the seeds, which are a great protein source. For this the naked seeded varieties are a real treat.

• TIPS FROM THE TOP OF THE WORLD •

Plums continued
      Shiro—standard, golden
      Starking Delicious®—semi-dwarf and standard
      Underwood—standard, hardy

NUTS

Almond
      Hall's Hardy
Black Walnut
      Plain
      Select
      Stark kwik-krop®
Butternut
Chinese Chestnut
English Walnut
      Carpathian Hardy
Filbert (Hazelnut)
Hickory Nut
Pecans

Nasturtium (Dwarf)
(1/10 size; detached
flowers, 1/3 size)

Cape Fear	Schley Paper Shell
Colby	Stark Surecrop®
Major	Starking Hardy Giant®
Missouri Giant	Stuart Paper Shell

ORNAMENTALS

Burbank Double Flowering Santa Rosa Peach®—also produces
   abundant small peaches
Crimson King Maple
Crownvetch Groundcover
Dogwood—4 selections, white, pink, red
Dwarf Burning Bush
French Lilacs—5 selections
Hydrangea—3 varieties
Privet—2 selections
Purple Leaf Maple
Radiant Flowering Crabapple
Red Honeysuckle
Roses
Silver Maple
Sugar Maple
Sweet Mock Orange—
   delightful scent
Weeping Willow

Early Hamburgh Parsley
(1/5 size)

Stokes Seeds
737 Main Street
P.O. Box 548
Buffalo, NY 14240

Stokes publishes a small catalog on newsprint, crammed with an amazing selection of vegetable and flower seeds. Their selection of carrots especially is incredible. The catalog is well organized, and there are few pictures. Many hybrids are featured as well as open pollinated varieties. Seeds are often treated so you should specify untreated seeds with your order. This is a good source for varieties suited to cooler, shorter seasons.

VEGETABLES

Beans
      Asparagus
      Fava
            Broad Windsor Long Pod
      French Horticultural Bush
      Kidney
            California Red
      Mung
      Romano Bush
      Royal Burgundy
      Soybean
            Fiskeby V—5-inch pods,
              70 days (Sweden)

Beets
      Albino White
      Cylindra
      Golden
      Little Egypt—34 days
      Little Mini-ball
      Winter Keeper

Cabbage—46 varieties including:
      Emerald Ace—61 days
      Evergreen Ballhead—storage
      Quick Green Storage—90 days
      Storage Red Short-stem

Carrots—31 varieties including:
      Baby Finger
      Coreless Amsterdam Nantes Forcing
      King Imperator—11 inches long
      Planet Round Miniature
      Royal Chantenay

Tarragon
(1/6 size;
detached leaf,
natural size)

Scarlet Coreless Nantes
Special Nantes 616
Super Nantes
Touchon Deluxe Nantes
Cauliflower
Stokes Early Abundance
Celeriac
Celtuce
Corn Salad
Cress and Watercress
Cucumbers
China
Double Yield Pickling
English Telegraph
Japanese Long Pickling
Lemon
Patio Pick Pickling
Sweet Slice
Escarole
Full Heart Batavian
Leeks
Alaska — winter hardy
Elephant
Giant Musselburgh
Titan — extra long
Unique — stores well
Lettuce
Butter King
Capitan — European greenhouse type
Grand Rapids Forcing
Ostinata — European greenhouse type
Parris Island Cos (Romaine)
Premier Great Lakes
Ruby
Slo Bolt
Melon
Cantaloupe
Delicious 51
Honeyloupe
Sugar Salmon
Watermelon
Allsweet
Charleston Grey
Citron — for preserving
Crimson Sweet
Sugar Baby

*Soy Bean
(1/8 size;
detached pods,
1/3 size)*

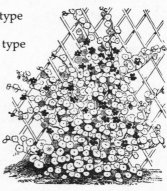

*Nasturtium,
or Indian Cress
(Tall or Large) (1/20 size;
detached flower,
1/5 size)*

Okra
       Perkins Mammoth Long Pod
Onions
       White Bunching—8 varieties including 2 60-day kinds
Parsley—7 selections including:
       Curlina—early mini-parsley for window boxes
Peanut
       Early Spanish—earliest maturing, for cool climates
Peas

Cameo—petit pois	Patriot
Lincoln	Sugar Snap
Little Sweetie—edible pod	Super Sweetpod
Novella	Tall Telephone

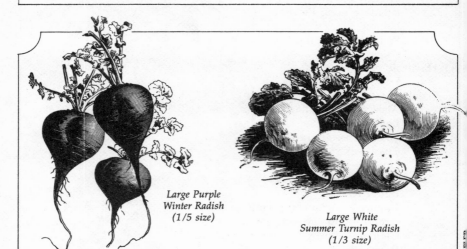

Large Purple
Winter Radish
(1/5 size)

Large White
Summer Turnip Radish
(1/3 size)

Radishes

Few vegetables come in as many beautiful colors and shapes as radishes: red, white, black, delicate pink, and sparkling red and white. Few crops grow as quickly and easily. Radishes can be harvested 3-6 weeks after sowing, about the time it takes parsley seed to sprout. "Winter" radishes like the lovely China Rose can be stored for winter use. Radish seed can be planted on approximate 2-inch centers by broadcasting 1 level tablespoon over 10 square feet. The yield is 20-40 pounds or more from 10 square feet. We also grow radishes as a cover crop because they produce as much or more organic matter per day than any other vegetable. As compost material, we harvest after they flower for a yield of 60-120 pounds from 10 square feet.

• TIPS FROM THE TOP OF THE WORLD •

Peppers—28 sweet pepper selections including:
    Earliest Red Sweet
    Early Canada Bell
    Golden California Wonder
    Italian Sweet
        Naples
        Super Shepherd
        Vinedale
    Pimento—6 selections in red and yellow
Peppers, Hot—8 selections including:
    Cayenne
    Hades
    Jalapeno
    Large Red Cherry
Radishes
    Chinese Rose
    Comet—good for warmer
      weather, stays crisp
    French Breakfast
Spinach
    Cold Resistant Savoy
Squash
    Acorn

        Jersey Golden
        Royal
        Table King Bush

Brown Netted, or Khiva,
Cucumber
(1/4 size)

    Buttercup
        Sweet Mama
    Butternut
        Ponca Baby—early
    Hubbard
        Golden
    Hungarian Mammoth
    Pumpkin
        Naked Seeded
        Small Sugar
        Spookie—for pies

    Scallop
    Sweet Potato
    Zucchini
        Gold Rush
        Greyzini
Tomatoes

Norwegian Savoy Cabbage
(1/12 size)

    Bush Beefsteak Early
    Cold Set Early
    Dwarf Champion—rose-pink, low acid, for tub culture

Tomatoes continued
       Golden Delight Dwarf—low acid
       Olympic Pink
       Pink Pearly Miniature
       Stakeless Miniature—deep red, 8 ounce
       Sub-Arctic Maxi Early—48 days
       Swift Early
       Vendor Fall Staking or Greenhouse

OTHER USEFUL PLANTS

Gourds—14 selections
Tobacco—4 selections

FLOWERS

All the flowers from Asters to Zinnias. They also offer Garden and Wildflower mixtures, seeds for ferns, cactus, ornamental grasses and a few trees like Ponderosa Pine.

SUPPLIES

Japanese Beetle Trap	Seeding Water Nozzle
Rubber Knee Pads	Soil Thermometer

Raspberries

Raspberries are a special, highly productive and tasty crop, but be sure you are ready for the work involved. They must be trellised from the start unless you grow freestanding varieties and each year roughly half the plant must be pruned back since berries are born on last year's canes. Though simple to understand, there is no avoiding a day of prickly work. Starts should be planted 4 feet apart in the center of beds 4 feet wide. One hundred square feet can produce 12-20 pounds. Black raspberries are higher in protein, calories and calcium than red ones.

• TIPS FROM THE TOP OF THE WORLD •

The Seed Finder

Sutton's Seeds Ltd.
Hele Road, Torquay
Devon, England TQ2-7QU

Sutton's offers choice flowers and vegetables including many cloche and rockery varieties. Descriptions are clear and honest and they include very good cultural notes. They are a good source of varieties that grow in cooler, damper climates.

VEGETABLES

Asparagus
    Sutton's Perfection—crowns
Beans
    Broad
        Aquadulce—for autumn sowing, very hardy
        Colossal—long podded
        Dwarf—early, good yields, can be grown under miniature
          greenhouses, 12 inches high
        Exhibition—long pod, very good yields
        Masterpiece Green Longpod
        Meteor—early, good yields
    French (Green)
        Climbing
            Coco Bi-Colour—pea bean
            Earliest of All—good yield over a long period
            Purple Podded—very good flavor
        Dwarf
            Chevrier Vert—disease resistant, good yield,
              can also be used for dry beans
            Kinghorn Wax—yellow
            Masterpiece—popular, early, continuous,
              good yields
          ★ The Prince—very good continuous yields, early
            Sprite Stringless—European, round podded
    Haricot
        Purley King—slow maturing for green or dry beans, dwarf
    Runner
        Best of All—red seeds, good yields, long season
      ★ Enorma—very good yields, good flavor
        Prizewinner—heavy yields
        Scarlet Emperor—very early
      ★ Sunset—pale pink flowers, early but will crop entire
          season, good flavor
Beets
    Avon Early—bolt resistant

Cabbage Family
    Broccoli
        Improved White Sprouting
        Italian Sprouting—excellent flavor
        Purple Sprouting
    Brussels Sprouts
        Bedford Fillbasket
        Bedford Winter Harvest—winter hardy
        Roodnerf Early Button—good yield, keeps well on stem
    Cabbage
        Best of All—early, savoy type
        Buderich—medium size autumn variety
        Holland Late Winter
        January King—savoy type
        Red Drumhead
    Cauliflower
        All the Year Round Early
        Angers No. 1
            Superb Early White
        Autumn Giant
            Superlative Protecting
        English Winter Progress—extremely hardy, over 20
          different cauliflowers are listed for different seaons
    Kale
        Thousand-Headed—hardy

Carrots
    Amsterdam Forcing—Amstel, for greenhouse culture
    Autumn King—early giant
    Chantenay Red Cored—favorite
    Early French Frame—for greenhouse culture
Celery
    American Green
    Giant Pink
        Unrivaled Pink
    Giant Red
    Golden Self-Blanching
    Solid White
Celtuce

Chicory
    Red Verona
    Sugar Loaf
    Whitloof
Cucumbers
    Butcher's Disease Resisting—for greenhouse culture
    Long Green—good yields

Movable two-sided
Mushroom-bed
(scale not shown)

The Seed Finder

Perfection—crops into autumn
Sigmadew—excellent flavor, for greenhouse culture
Telegraph Improved—for greenhouse culture
Venlo Pickling

Eggplant
Long Purple

Greens
Corn Salad
Cress
Dandelion
Endive
Moss Curled
Mustard
White
Parsley
Claudia—double curled, hardy
Common—flat-leaved
Hamburg—for parsnip-type roots
Moss Curled
★Paramount—dark green, very hardy, slow bolting
Purslane
Spinach
Greenmarket—winter hardy, good yield, slow bolter
Long-standing Round—early, good yield if keep picking
outer leaves

Leeks
Autumn Mammoth
Early Market
Winter Crop

Lettuce
Butterhead
All the Year Round—slow to bolt
Fortune—quick growing
Sigmaball—stands in condition over a long period
Crisp Hearted
Windermere—quick maturing, slow bolting,
drought tolerant
Forcing Varieties
Dandie—quick maturing, for heated greenhouses
Klock—for slightly heated cold greenhouses
Kwick—for cold greenhouses
May Queen—quick maturing, red-tinged, for cold frames
Romaine (Cos)
Little Gem—quick maturing
Lobjoits Green—dark green
Winter Density—dwarf

*Mushrooms
grown in a tub
(scale not shown)*

continued

Rhubarb

(Rheum hybridum)

Rhubarb, originally from Mongolia, makes great pies and produces much more quickly if you begin it from roots. One person we know placed a wooden barrel with the top and bottom removed around the plants when they were 12 inches high to encourage additional growth. Plant roots 24 inches apart where they can remain permanently. Harvests can be 10 pounds or more from a 10 square foot patch. Cut off green parts when harvesting. They are poisonous.

Rhubarb Stalks (1/7 size)

• TIPS FROM THE TOP OF THE WORLD •

Lettuce continued

> Winter Varities
>> Arctic King—extremely hardy
>> Imperial Winter—very hardy

Melons
> Cantaloupe
>> Charantais—French, good yield, orange-scarlet flesh
>> Ogden—small, half-hardy
> Emerald Gem—green fleshed
> Hero of Lockinge—white fleshed
> Superlative—scarlet fleshed

Mushroom Spawn
> Darlington's—white buttons

Okra—long green

Onions
> Ailsa Craig Selected—large, popular
> Barletta—for pickling
> Brunswick—red
> ★Budfordshire Champion—long keeper, heavy crop, ripens early
> Extra Early Kaizuka
> Paris Silver Skin—very early
> Rijnsburger—yellow skin, white flesh
> Senshyu Semi-Globe Yellow
> Solidity—autumn variety
> Sturon—round, good flavor and keeping qualities
> White Lisbon—winter hardy
> White Spanish

The Seed Finder

Parsnip
  Improved Hollow Crown
  Tender and True
  White Gem
Peas
  Continental
      Gullivert (Petit Pois) — French, heavy yields
      Purple Podded
      Tall White Sugar
  Early Varieties
    ★ Feltham First — earliest commercial variety, dwarf, late
        autumn or early spring, good for mini-greenhouses too,
        18 inches high
      Little Marvel
      Meteor — extremely hardy for very early sowing
  Maincrop
      Lord Chancellor — very good yields
  Second Early
      Chieftain — excellent flavor
      Miracle — very good yields
      Onward — most popular, stress tolerant

Peppers (Capsicum)
  Worldbeater — green, sweet

Potatoes
  Majestic — maincrop
  Sutton's Foremost — early, white, oval

Radishes
  China Rose Winter
  French Breakfast — succulent
  Long Black Spanish Winter
  Round Black Spanish Winter
  Saxa — red, for forcing
Salsify
Scorzonera
Shallot
  Giant Yellow
  Hative de Niort
Squash
  Bush Table Queen
  Custard Yellow (Patty Pan)
  Golden Hubbard
  Long Green Striped
  Long White Trailing
  Pumpkin
      Hundredweight — very large, good storer

*Alleaume Dwarf
Cauliflower
(scale not shown)*

Tomatoes

 Ailsa Craig-Leader—hardy, early, greenhouse or outdoor
★ Alicante—early, for greenhouse and outdoor culture
 The Amateur—early bush type
 Golden Sunrise—yellow, greenhouse or outdoor
 Harbinger—early, heavy cropper, greenhouse or outdoor
 Marmande—very good flavor, for outdoors
 Moneymaker—very heavy yields, greenhouse or outdoor
 Potentate
  Best of All—for greenhouse and outdoor culture
 Primabel—good flavor and yields, bush type
★ Tangella—tangerine color, early

Turnips and Rutabagas

★ Golden Ball—dwarf yellow, keeps well in ground or storage
★ Golden Perfection—golden early
 Jersey Navet—greenhouse or outdoor
 Milan White—very early, dwarf, greenhouse or outdoor

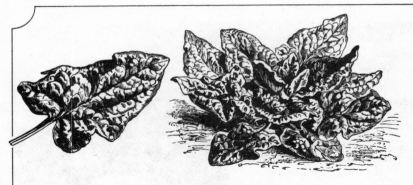

Late-seeding, or Long-stander, Spinach (1/6 size)

Spinach

Spinach is often hard for people to grow. Be sure to plant in-season.
Spinach does best in the cooler spring and autumn. You can sow
spinach directly in the soil on 4- or 5-inch centers (2 seeds per center
because of low germination), though we've had good results trans-
planting seedlings. Sigmaleaf, from Sutton's, sounds good. It has a
long harvest and is slow to go to seed. For a smoother leaved spinach
try Soshu from Redwood City. For best results harvest outside leaves
as they mature. Yield is about 10 pounds from 10 square feet.

Turnips continued

      Rutabagas (Swedes)
           Manchurian (Bronze-top)—good storer
           Sutton's Western Perfection (Purple-top)—fast grower,
              good storer
      Snowball—early, mild
      Vetch's Red Globe—red tops, white flesh

USEFUL PLANTS

Tobacco
      Mont Calma Brown

FRUIT

Alpine Strawberries
      Alexandra—Swiss everbearing
      Baron Solemacher—special flavor
      Fraise de Bois—wild everbearing
      Red Alpine—autumn bearing

*Early Nantes Carrot
(1/5 size)*

FLOWERS

Acroclinium
      Strawflower
Adonis Aestivalis
      Pheasant's Eye
Ageratum
Agrostemma—for dry areas, cut flower
Alyssum—white, rose and purple
      Oriental Night—deep purple
      Wonderland—deep red
Alyssum Saxatile—taller, perennial alyssum
      Golden Queen—bright yellow flowering
      Silver Queen—pale yellow
Anchusa—2 dazzling selections
Anemone
      De Caen
      St. Brigid
Antirrhinum—Snapdragons a specialty!
  46 selections including dwarf and
  rust resistant varieties in every color
Arabis Alpina—Rock Cress
Asclepras Curassavica
      Blood Flower
      Milkweed

*Fennel Flower
(flower and
seed-vessel,
1/2 size)*

Atriplex Hortensis Rubra
     Red Mountain Spinach—foliage plant
Aubrieta—rockery flower in rose and violet
Auricula—rockery flower, hardy in severe winters
Asters—21 selections, doubles, singles, dwarfs
     Duchess Mixed
     Ostrich Plume Mixture
Balsam
     Camellia—Flowered Mix
     Extra Dwarf Tom Thumb Mix
Bartonia Aurea—quick flowering annual with large bright
  yellow flowers
Begonia
     Fibrous—free flowering ground cover type plant
     Tuberous—great in hanging baskets
Cabbage—Ornamental
Cacalia Coccinea—Tassel Flower, vivid-orange scarlet flowers
Calceolaria—Slipper Flower, 3 selections
     Perfection Mixed
Calendula—English or Pot Marigold
     Art Shades—in apricot, flame, pale orange, primrose and cream
     Geisha Girl
     Golden King
    ★Gypsy Festival—gorgeous
     Lemon Queen
     Orange King
     Prince of Orange—with black centers
     Radio—cutting variety
Canterbury Bell
     Bells of Holland—dwarf
     Sutton's Cup and Saucer in Pink, White, Blue
Carnation
     Dwarf Fragrance—Perennial
     Sutton's Chabaud Giant
     Vanguard—exquisitely scented,
        bizarre and fancy flowers
Celosia Plumosa
     Fairy Fountains—new color range
     Fire Feather
     Golden Feather
Cerastium—Snow in Summer
Chrysanthemum—10 selections
Cineraria—7 selections
Clarkia
Clary—unusual colored leaves for
  flower arranging and drying

Blood-red Flat Italian
Onion
(1/3 size)

Cleome—Spider Flower
Cobaca Scandens—Cup and Saucer Plant, rapid climber
Coleus—7 selections
Coreopsis
    Calliopsis—Annual varieties in range of colors
    Perennials with Golden Yellow Flowers
Dahlias—12 selections
Delphinium
    Connecticut Yankees
    Mount Everest—snowy white
    Rich Blue
    Sutton's Chinensis—Blue Butterfly
Dimorphotheca
    Giant Orange
    Glistening White
Edelweiss
Felicia Bergeriana
Freesias—Royals Mixed
Gaillardia
Gavra Lindheimeri
Geranium—16 varieties from seed
Geum
    Lady Stratheden
    Mrs. Bradshaw
Godetia
Helianthus—Sunflower
    Giant Yellow
    Sunburst
Helichrysum—Strawflower
    Bright Bikini—dwarf, color range
    Dwarf Mixed
    Hot Bikini—intense red flowers, dwarf
    Sutton's Tall
Heliotrope
    Marine—violet purple flowers, heavily scented
Honesty—Lunaria or Money Plant
Larkspur—7 selections
    Sutton's Stock Flowered
Lathyrus—Everlasting Sweet Pea
Lavatera—Mallow
    Mont Blanc
    Silver Cup
    Sutton's Loveliness
Lavender—Munstead Dwarf
Liatris—Blazing Star
Limnanthes Douglasii—Poached Egg Flower—easy annual

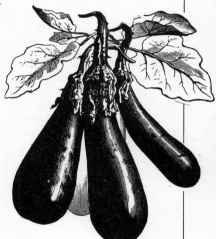

*Long Purple
Eggplant
(1/5 size)*

*Yellow Custard Marrow
(1/6 size)*

*Elector's-cap, or Custard, Marrow
(1/6 size)*

*Italian Vegetable Marrow
(1/8 size)*

Squash, Summer

Summer squash are all the soft varieties such as zucchini, yellow crookneck and Patty Pan. Squash and pumpkins crossbreed quite easily. If you have ever planted seed you saved from the previous year you will have noticed odd and even exotic looking fruits. Many are quite delicious and useful. To save seed from a small garden, plants must be isolated. The highest yielding squash is still green zucchini, yielding 32-48 pounds from 10 square feet. Plant 18 inches apart. Crookneck and Patty Pan are planted 15 inches apart. From 10 square feet Crookneck will yield 7-15 pounds and Patty Pan will yield 15-31 pounds.

• TIPS FROM THE TOP OF THE WORLD •

Flowers continued

Linaria
      Fairy Bouquet
Linum — Blue Flax and Scarlet Flax
Lithops — Living Stones — exquisite small succulents
Lobelia — compact varieties, the best colors trailing varieties
  in blue/red/purple
Love-Lies-Bleeding — long crimson tassels
Lychnis
      Arkwrightii
      Chalcedonica — Jerusalem Cross
Marigolds — African, Afro-French and French types, 49 selections
Meconopsis
      Tibetan Poppy — 3 feet, brilliant blue flowers
Mignonette — sweet-scented
Myosotis — Forget-me-not — 5 selections

The Seed Finder

Nasturtiums—9 selections
Nicandra Physaloides—Shoo-fly Plant
Nicotiana—Flowering Tobacco, 9 selections in white, red, rose,
   lemon yellow, pink, lime, crimson
Pansy—22 selections
Passion Flower
Petunia—40 selections
Phacelia
Phlox Drummondii
Physalis—Chinese Lanterns

Poppies
   Hardy Annuals
      Pacony Flowered
      Sutton's Shirley
   Hardy Perennial
      Alpine Mixed
      Oriental
      San Remo—Iceland
      Sutton's Large-Flowered Special Mixture

Broad-leaved, or Batavian,
Endive
(1/8 size)

Portulaca—Sutton's Improved Double Mixed, rose, scarlet, orange,
   purple, white
Primulas—of all types
Ranunculus
Rhodanthe—dried flower, daisy-like, rose colored
Rock Cistus—Sun Rose

Rudbeckia
   Gloriosa Daisy Mixed
   Irish Eyes—yellow petals and green center
   Marmalade
   Rustic Dwarfs Mixed

Salvia—9 selections
   Spectacular—mix of 10 colors
Saponaria
Saxifrage
Scabious
Schizanthus
Silene, Schafta
Smilax
Statice—dried flower sprays in yellow,
   pink, lavender and blue
Stocks—27 selections including summer,
   winter, autumn and spring flowering;
   also night-scented strains
Strelitzia—Bird of Paradise

Witloof, or Large
Brussels Chicory
(1/3 size)

Sweet Pea—39 beautiful selections in white, cream, ivory, salmon,
  scarlet, carmine, crimson, maroon, purple, mauve, lavender, blue,
  pink, rose and cerise
    Cream Beauty
    Knee Hi Mixed Colors
    Old Fashioned Scented
Sweet Rocket—Hesperis Matronalis, favorite Old English flower
Sweet William—11 selections
Tagetes Signata—lovely little mounds
    Golden Gem
    Lemon Gem
    Paprika
    Tangerine Gem
Thunbergia—Black-eyed Susan, climbing vine
Torenia
Tropacolum Canariense—Canary Creeper
Valerian—Red
Verbascum
    Phoeniceum Choice Mixed
    Sutton's Silver Spire
Verbena—Giant and Dwarf in a rainbow of colors
Veronica
    Shirley Blue
    Speedwell
Viola Odorata—Fragrant Sweet Violet
Violas
Virginian Creeper
Virginian Stock
★ Viscaria
    Sutton's Brilliant Mixture
Wallflowers—fragrant and easy to grow, 30 selections with a color
  range through scarlet and pink to orange and yellow
    Sutton's Persian Carpet—pastel shades
Zinnias—18 selections

Blunt-rooted
Guerande Carrot
(scale not shown)

124   *The Seed Finder*

FLOWERING BULBS

Acidanthera
Anemone
Begonia—Double Tuberous, 13 selections
  ★ Giant Double Strain Mixed—beautiful shades of white, yellow,
    salmon, rose, scarlet, flame, orange and crimson
Dahlia Tubers—44 selections
    Edinburgh—crimson-purple tipped with white
    Extravaganza—orange-red cactus type
    Helga—crimson semi-cactus
Freesias
Gladioli—50 selections including miniatures
Lilies—19 selections
    African Queen
    Brandywine
    Bright Star
    Fire King
    Golden Splendor
    Green Dragon
    Tiger Lily
Nerine
Ranunculus

Detached Branch

ORNAMENTALS

Flowering shrubs from seed
    Arbutus
    Broom
        Spanish
        White
    Chaenomeles—Japanese Quince
    Cotoneaster
    Hypericum
Lawn Mixes
    Greenglade—for shady areas
    Summer Day—lush and springy
    Summer Play—hard wearing
Plus Sutton's Organic Turf Dressing

Summer Savory
(1/8 size)

Vermont Bean Seed Co.
Garden Lane
Bomoseen, VT 05732

Vermont Bean Seed Co. specializes in beans and offers a great selection of this staple crop. Evaluations are honest with no hype. Information is clear and helpful. Packets are generous. They also offer vegetable and wildflower seeds.

VEGETABLES

Beans
    Dried Beans
        Black Turtle
        Fava
        Flageollet
        French Horticultural
        Garbanzo (Chick Pea)
        Great Northern White
        Jacob's Cattle
        Mung
        Navy Pea
        Pink
        Pinto
        Red Kidney
        Red Mexican
        Red Peanut
        Soldier—maroon marking, cooler climate
        Swedish Brown
        Vermont Cranberry
        White Kidney
        Yellow Eye
    Green Beans
        Black Valentine—heirloom seed
        Blue Lake—bush and pole
        Blue Ribbon—pole
        Bluecrop—bush
        Bountiful Stringless—bush
        Burpee's Stringless Green Pod—bush
        Dade—pole
        Daisy Bean—bush, pods set high above foliage
        Genuine Cornfield—pole
        Greencrop—bush
        Kentucky Wonder—bush and pole
        Kentucky Wonder White Pole
        Missouri Runner—pole

Chives
(1/8 size;
separate stem,
1/4 size)

Oregon Giant Paul Bunyan—pole
Provider—bush
Rattlesnake—pole, drought resistant
Romano—bush and pole
Royalty Burgundy Purple Pod—bush
Scarlet Runner—pole
Slenderette Snap—bush
Stringless Green Pod—bush
Sulphur—rare heirloom bean
Tendercrop—bush
Tendergreen Improved—bush
Tennessee Green—bush
Thomas' Famous White Dutch
    Runner—grows up to 10 feet,
    hummingbirds love flowers, rare
Top Crop—bush
White Half-Runner
Wren's Egg—pole
Lima Beans
Burpee's Improved—bush
Christmas—pole, beautiful red striping
Dixie Speckled Butter Pea—bush
Dreer's Improved—pole
Florida Speckled Butterbean—pole
Fordhook®—bush
Fordhook® 'Baby'—bush
Henderson's—bush
Jackson Wonder—bush
King of the Garden—pole
Southern Running Butterbean—pole
Thorogreen—bush
Yellow Snap Beans
Cherokee Wax
Earlywax Golden Yellow
Golden Wax Improved
Kentucky Wonder Yellow Wax Pole
Pencil Pod Wax
Resistant Kinghorn Wax
Celtuce—can be used like lettuce and celery
Cucumber
White Wonder—old fashioned, white

St. Valery Carrot
(1/5 size)

Greens
    Garland—aromatic, edible-leaved Chrysanthemum
    Mustard—Florida Broadleaf
    Parsley—Forest Green
    Santoh—oriental, celery-like
    Seven Top Turnip Greens
    Taisai—loose-leaved Chinese cabbage
Melons
    Cantaloupe
        Far North—for cool climates
    Watermelon
        Winterkeeper—can be stored for several months
Onions
    He-ski-ko Long White Bunching
    White Sweet Spanish Jumbo
    Yellow Stuttgart Sets—Dutch

Hubbard Squash
(1/6 size)

Squash, Winter

Contrary to logic, winter squash are not grown in winter. They are the hard-shelled squash—acorn, hubbard, butternut, spaghetti, and pumpkin—that are grown in summer and stored for winter use. We grow a lot. We rarely have time to can but can count on winter stores of squash and potatoes and fresh chard. Squash seeds are toasted 5-10 minutes in a skillet or moderate oven and eaten shell and all. Spaghetti squash must be harvested when shell is white and just beginning to turn yellow. Older squashes will be starchy. Spaghetti squash will store about 6 weeks. After that some turn slightly bitter. Plant winter squash on 18-, 24- or 30-inch centers according to the size of the squash. Yield is 10-20 pounds or more from 10 square feet.

— • TIPS FROM THE TOP OF THE WORLD • —

The Seed Finder

Peas
    Alaska—55 days, the earliest
    Almota—disease resistant
    Cowpeas
        Black Eye Bean (Queen Anne)   Crimson (Arkansas Pea)
        Brown Crowders   Mississippi Silver
        Chinese Red Bean   Pink Eye Purple Hull

    Dwarf Telephone
    Early Frosty
    Edible Pod
        Dwarf Grey Sugar   Oregon Sugar
        Dwarf White Sugar   Sugar Rae "Snap"
        Green Sugar   Sugar Snap
        Mammoth Melting   Sweet Snap

    Freezonian
    Green Arrow
    Hustler
    Kosta
    Lacy Lady—almost leafless,
        tendrils hold bushs erect
    Laxton's Progress
    Lincoln
    Little Marvel
    Mammoth Early Canner
    Perfection Dark Green
    Petite Pois—tiny French
    Progress #9—earliest, 60 days
    Superb Early Bird
    Superfection—good yields and taste
    Tall Telephone or Alderman
    Thomas Laxton
    Wando
Peppers
    Cayenne Long Slim
    Hungarian Yellow Wax
    Jalapeno M
    Mild California (Paprika)
    Red Cherry Small

Potatoes, sweet
    Centennial
    ★ Porto Rico—bush
Shallots—Extra Select Premium
    Grade Bulbs

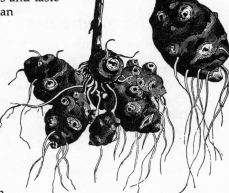

Jerusalem Artichoke
(1/5 size)

Squash
    Pumpkins
        Big Moon
        Hungarian Mammoth
        Jack O'Lantern
        Kentucky Large Field
        Small Sugar Pie
Tomato
    Sunray—yellow, wilt resistant

WILDFLOWERS

Brilliant Mixture   Low Growing Mixture
Cutflower Mixture   Pastel Mixture

TOOLS AND SUPPLIES

Liquid Seaweed
Seaweed Meal
Vermont Maple Syrup

May Queen

La Constante

Red Alpine

Strawberries

Strawberries are always a favorite. Some varieties will grow just about anywhere in the world. Friends who have kept records tell us their 100 sq. feet of strawberry plants can yield 30-40 gallons. Buy 1-year-old plants in January and set out on 12-inch centers. The highest yields will be in the second and third years after planting. Expect 8-16 pounds from 10 square feet. Replant the growing area by the fifth year with new "runners" taken from your old plants. Nourse Farms specializes in flavorful strawberry plants in large quantities.

British Queen

© 1982, 1983 BY JOHN JEAVONS AND ROBIN LELER

● TIPS FROM THE TOP OF THE WORLD ●

Tree Crops ★
Rt. 1, Box 44B
Covelo, CA 95428

Tree Crops is our favorite source of trees. Stock currently varies immensely each year. Their trees are the healthiest we have ever planted. Catalog is tiny—sending 50¢ or a stamped envelope with your request will help a lot. Fruit trees are especially suited to Northern California.

APPLES

Available as standard or semi-dwarf
- Arkansas Black
- Bellflower
- Blenheim
- Cox Orange Pippin
- Golden Delicious
- Granny Smith
- Gravenstein
- Jonathan
- King of Tompkin
- McIntosh
- Mutsu
- Newtown
- Northern Spy
- Sierra Beauty
- Spitzenberg
- Stayman
- Waltana
- Winesap
- Winter Banana

RARE APPLES

Limited supply available:
- American Beauty
- Ashmead Kernel
- Belle de Boskop
- Ben Davis
- Bentley
- Black Gilliflower
- Blue Pearmain
- Canada Reinette
- English Beauty

Red Currant Tomato Branch, 1/3 size

Detached Fruit

Rare Apples continued
- Fameuse
- Golden Russet
- Hubbandston
- Jonadel
- King
- King David
- Lady
- Mother
- Oldenburg
- Oliver
- Peack's Pleasant
- Rhode Island Greening
- Ribston Pippin
- Roxbury Russet
- Sixteen Ounce
- Smokehouse
- Sops of Wine
- Sutton Beauty
- Swaar
- Wealthy
- White Pippin
- Yellow Transparent

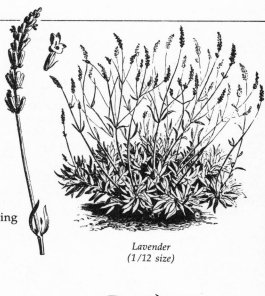

Lavender
(1/12 size)

PEARS

- Anjou
- Bartlett
- Bevrre Giffard
- Bosc
- Comice
- Flemish Beauty
- Hardy
- Seckel
- Winter Nellis

Greengage, or
Yellow Plum,
Tomato
(scale not shown)

PLUMS

Damson
French Prune—delicious fresh or dried, also called "sugar plum"
Green Gage
Imperial Prune
Pearl
Santa Rosa

HEDGES AND WINDBREAKS

Very inexpensive seedlings
    Basket Willow
    Black Locust
    Black Mulberry
    Common Lilac
    Common Plum
   ★ Honey Locust
    Manchu Cherry
    Pyracantha Coccinea
    Rosa Rugosa—a rose that makes a dense hedge
    Russian Olive
    Scotch Broom
    Siberian Crabapple
    Siberian Elm
    Sweetbriar (Rosa eglanteria)
    White Spanish Broom
    Vitex negundo incisa

SPECIAL HONEYPLANTS

Anise Hyssop
Blue Sage
Chivirico
Golden Honeyplant
Motherwort
Mountain Mint
Purple Loosestrife

Late Hamburgh
Parsley
(1/5 size)

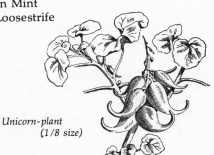

Unicorn-plant
(1/8 size)

C. v. d. P.

Sunflowers

What garden is complete without these beautiful giants. We can hardly stop our daughters from growing them since the 3-year-old won $2.50 at the county fair for a large one she proudly grew herself. The dried seeds are a good protein source for birds and people and supply a good cooking oil, though the extraction process is a good bit of work. Plant seeds on 24-inch centers. Yield is 2½-5 pounds of hulled, dried seeds from 10 square feet.

Wilson Plant Sales
505 S. Indiana St.
Roachdale, IN 46172

This company prints a slim catalog focusing on geraniums. We especially enjoy the scented geraniums. The leaves, when rubbed, give off wonderful scents. The rose-scented one is an old favorite. The scent is delicious. Leaves are reportedly used to flavor cakes, jellies and teas. The plant is hardy and very easy to grow with lacy leaves and lovely, tiny, orchid-pink flowers. It is a star plant around patios or gates. It grows 3-4 feet tall. Other scented geraniums are usually shorter.

SCENTED GERANIUMS

There are many more than those listed here, though they are very hard to find and rarely grown.

Apple
Eucalyptus
Lemon
Lime
Peppermint
Rose
} strong, recognizable scents

Apricot
Cinnamon
Ginger
Nutmeg
} less recognizable scents but still lovely plants

OTHERS

African Violets—including trailing types
Geraniums—with many unusual flowers
Houseplants—many flowering types
Miniature Geraniums—in all colors
Vining Ivy Leaf Geraniums—great for hanging baskets or ground
    cover. Mostly pinks and reds, some white and violet.

Woodruff
(1/10 size plus
detached flowers)

Dave Wilson Nursery
4306 Santa Fe Ave.
Hughson, CA 95326

Dave Wilson specializes in fruit and nut trees, offering the latest and most popular varieties, especially "Zaiger" genetically dwarfed fruits recommended for home orchards. Especially valuable are their detailed evaluations of each variety's performance in 149 different zones encompassing all of the United States. Their trees are available at many key nurseries, but no longer by mail order. Check with your local nursery person.

FRUITS

Apples
- Anna—for warm climates
- Beverly Hills—Southern California
- Dorsett Golden—for warm climates
- Empire—McIntosh type for warmer climates
- Garden Delicious Zaiger Genetic Dwarf
- Golden Delicious
- Granny Smith
- Gravenstein—Best in the West
- McIntosh—best in cold climates
- Mutsu
- Prima—scab resistant
- Priscilla—disease resistant for humid climates
- Red Delicious (Bisbee Spur)
- Yellow Newton Pippin

Apples are offered on four different root stocks—differences are detailed clearly in the catalog.

Apricots
- Blenheim (Royal)
- Flora Gold—consistent producer
- ★ Garden Annie Zaiger Genetic Dwarf
- Gold Kist—for warmer climates
- Moorpark
- Tilton

Cherries
- Bing—best flavor
- Black Tartarian
- Garden Bing Zaiger Genetic Dwarf
- Lambert—excellent flavor
- Larian—excellent flavor
- Montmorency—for pies
- North Star—hardy pie cherry for northern climates

Rainier—yellow sweet cherry
Stella
Van—very close to Bing but hardier
4-N-1—Rainier, Larian, Bing and Van on one tree
3-N-1—Larian, Bing, Van
2-N-1—Bing and Van
2-N-1—Lambert and Van
2-N-1—Bing and Larian
2-N-1—Rainier and Van

Figs
Black Mission
Conadria

Grapes
Campbell's Early—purple
Cardinal—dark red
Delaware—red skin with light green flesh
Eastern Concord—blue-black
European Wine
Cabernet Sauvignon—red
French Colombard—white
Pinot Chardonnay—white
Ruby Cabernet—red
White Riesling
Zinfandel—red
Fredonia—black
Lady Finger—green
Muscat of Alexandria—green
Niagara—greenish yellow
Seedless
Black Monukka—reddish black
Flame—red
Perlette—light green
Thompson—greenish white
White Diamond

Kiwi
California Male
Hayward Female

*Horse-radish
(1/5 size)*

*Greek, or Athenian,
Cucumber
(1/5 size)*

*Cherry Tomato
branch (1/3 size)*

Apple-shaped Red, or Hathaway's Excelsior

*Pear-shaped, or
Fig, Tomato
(1/3 size)*

Tomatoes

It is difficult to recommend any particular tomato. Everyone has their own fiercely defended favorite. We like the sweet cherry tomatoes and use the pear-shaped canning types for fresh eating, cooking and drying. There are also beautiful orange, yellow and white tomatoes, the giant Beefsteak types which require long hot summers to ripen properly, sub-arctic tomatoes for cooler seasons and greenhouse varieties. Unless you are growing hybrids, save some seed. Your own tomatoes will grow sweeter each year. Though fruits ripen faster when the plants are pruned or pinched back, slightly higher yields are obtained from unpruned ones. The small cherry tomatoes are transplanted onto 18-inch centers, regular size tomatoes on 21-inch centers and the larger types 24 inches apart. Yields are 19-42 pounds from 10 square feet. We set plants out over the entire bed with an 8-foot stake pushed 18 inches into the soil next to each one, tying the plant loosely 9 inches above ground. When the plants are about 18 inches high, we run a string around the outer stakes to keep the plants from falling into the path. As the plants grow we repeat the string around the outside about every 9 inches. This creates a simple, low-maintenance framework within which the plants support each other.

© 1982, 1983 BY JOHN JEAVONS AND ROBIN LELER

• TIPS FROM THE TOP OF THE WORLD •

The Seed Finder

Nectarines
    Desert Dawn—for warmer climates
    Early Sweet
    Fantasia
    Garden Delight—Zaiger genetic dwarf
    Garden King—Zaiger genetic dwarf
    Golden Beauty—Zaiger genetic dwarf
    Goldmine
    Independence
    Mericrest
    2W68W Zaiger—cold hardy
Peaches
    August Pride Zaiger—for warmer climates
    Desert Gold—for warmer climates
    Dixon
    Fantastic Elberta
    Fay Elberta
    Garden Gold—Zaiger genetic dwarf
    Garden Sun—Zaiger genetic dwarf
    Giant Babcock
    Gold Dust—for warmer climates
    Honey Babe—Zaiger genetic dwarf
    Indian Free
    J.H. Hale
    July Elberta
    Loring
    Madison—cold hardy
    Mid Pride Zaiger—for warmer climates
    Nectar
    Redhaven
    Ranger
    Redskin
    Reliance—cold hardy
    Rio Oso Gem
    Royal Gold Zaiger—for warmer climates
    Sentinel
    Vetran
Pears

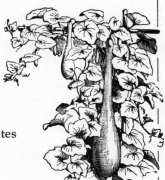

Club Gourd
(1/15 size)

Ayers	Magress	Asian, also called
Bartlett	Moonglow	pear-apples:
Bosc	Orient	Chojuro
Comice	Seckel	Shinseiki
D'Anjou	Sensation	20th Century
Kieffer	Tyson	Ya Li

Persimmons
    Fuyu—hardy and beautiful tree, delicious non-astringent fruit
    Hachiya
Plums
    Cherry—plums
        Delight
        Sprite
    Green Gage
    Italian
    Mariposa
    Queen Anne—mahogany skin and amber flesh
    Santa Rosa
    Satsuma
    Stanley
    Weeping Santa Rosa
    Wickson
Plumcots
    ★Plum Parfait Zaiger Semi-dwarf
Pomegranates
    Wonderful
Quince
    Pineapple
Strawberries
    Fort Laramie—cold hardy, everbearing
    Guardian
    Ozark Beauty—adaptable, everbearing
    Quinault—everbearing
    Sequoia—June-bearing, for mild winters

NUT TREES

Almonds
    ★Garden Prince Zaiger Dwarf
    Mission
    Nonpareil
    Price
Chestnuts
    Colossal
Filberts
    Barcelona
    Daviana
    Hall's Giant

Pecans
    Cheyenne
    Choctaw
    Kiowa
    Mohawk
    Tejas
    Western Schley
    Wichita
Walnuts
    Ambassador
    Chandler
    Franquette
    Hartley

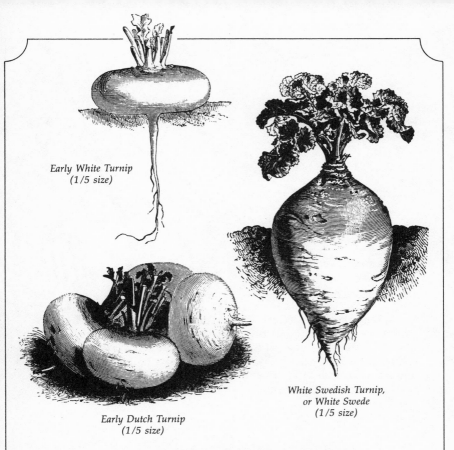

Early White Turnip
(1/5 size)

Early Dutch Turnip
(1/5 size)

White Swedish Turnip,
or White Swede
(1/5 size)

Turnips and Rutabagas

Turnips are tasty raw as well as cooked. We especially like rutabagas, called Swedes in England. Try some thin slices with your favorite dip. We find they are sweeter grown in biointensive raised beds and store fairly well for winter use. Turnips are planted on 3-inch centers and rutabagas 6 inches apart. The yield from 10 square feet is 20-36 pounds of turnips or up to 40 pounds of rutabagas.

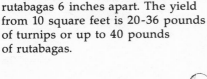

White Strap-leaved
American Stone Turnip
(1/5 size)

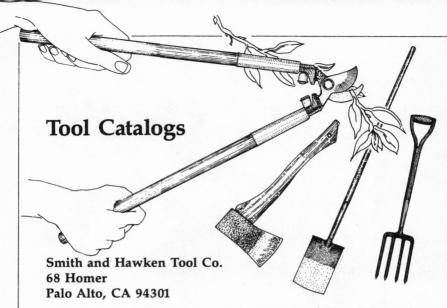

Tool Catalogs

Smith and Hawken Tool Co.
68 Homer
Palo Alto, CA 94301

Smith and Hawken offers finely crafted garden tools. They are expensive but sturdy and beautiful. Spades and forks have elegant wooden D-handles. A good working combination is a medium weight spade and a heavy duty fork. They also offer exquisite smaller forks and spades for children, the perfectly balanced Haws watering cans, pruners, and many other tools.

Walter Nicke's Garden Talk
P.O. Box 667G
Hudson, NY 12534

catalog 50¢

Nicke's is a unique source of garden aids, many imported from England. Especially useful we find are the Spyn-Gydes. They sit in the ground and magically guide hoses around the corners of garden beds without knocking over the plants. They also have fine garden baskets or trugs, flower snips, garden labels, English thatched roof bird houses and other treasures.

Drawings on this page courtesy of the Smith and Hawken Tool Co. and Walter Nicke's Garden Talk.

Bibliography

VEGETABLES

How To Grow More Vegetables Than You Ever Thought Possible On Less Land Than You Can Imagine, by John Jeavons. How to give your plants the richest garden to grow in, resulting in vigor, abundance, flavor and pleasure. The greatly expanded third edition is available for $7.95, plus $.75 postage and handling, from Ecology Action, 2225 El Camino, Palo Alto, CA 94306 and Ten Speed Press, P.O. Box 7123, Berkeley, CA 94707. (California residents add sales tax.)

The Vegetable Garden, by M.M. Vilmorin. Over 600 pages of highly detailed cultural directions and engravings, nearly 100 years old. Paperback available for $11.95, plus $.75 postage and handling, from Ten Speed Press. Hardcover available for $16.50 including postage and handling, from Jeavons-Leler Press, 5798 Ridgewood Road, Willits, CA 95490. (California residents add sales tax.)

SEED SAVING

Growing and Saving Vegetable Seeds, by Marc Rogers. Available from Garden Way, Charlotte, VT 05445.

Growing Garden Seeds, by Robert Johnston, Jr. Available for $2.50 from Johnny's Selected Seeds, Albion, ME 04910.

Vegetable and Herb Seed Growing For the Gardener and Small Farmer, by Douglas C. Miller. We find this to be a very useful and easy-to-understand guide to seed collection. Self-published. Available for $3.50 from Bullkill Creek Publishing, Hersey, MI 49639.

Vegetable Seed Production, by Craig Dremann. A 6-page mimeograph with seed collection and cleaning details. An expanded version is planned. $.50 from Redwood City Seed Co., P.O. Box 360, Redwood City, CA 94064.

FLOWERS

Crockett's Flower Garden, by James Crockett. Great photos and experienced cultural notes. Little, Brown and Co., Boston, MA. 1981.

How To Make Cut Flowers Last, by Victoria R. Kasperski. Great guide from William Morrow & Co., New York. 1956.

FRUIT

Citrus, by Richard Ray and Lance Walheim. Available from HP Books for $7.95 plus postage and handling, P.O. Box 5367, Tucson, AZ 85703.

How To Prune Fruit Trees, by Sanford R. Martin. The best and simplest book on pruning for West Coast gardeners. Published by the author, 10535 Las Lunitas Ave., Tujunga, CA 91042.

Western Fruit, Berries and Nuts, by Lance Walheim and Robert L. Stebbins. Glossy color photos and excellent coverage. $7.95 plus postage and handling from HP Books.

*Caper-bush (1/10 size;
detached branch,
1/3 size)*

Why Not Hybrids?

We like and use open-pollinated varieties, not hybrids, because:

1.   Rarely will hybrids reproduce true to type, so you cannot save seed from them.

2.   Hybrid seed is much more costly because of the custom pollinating involved.

3.   Use of hybrids on a large scale leads to genetic uniformity in crops. Less diversity makes crops more vulnerable to certain disease and insect problems.

4.   Hybrids often depend on increased water and fertilizer use for their "vigor." Open-pollinated varieties often have adapted to wider temperature ranges and some have proven themselves in less than optimal conditions such as drought.

5.   We feel it is important for people to retain the ability to be self-reliant. It is unfortunate when the 200-300 varieties of rice once grown in Sri Lanka are replaced by a handful of hybrids.

6.   Increased yield is often found to be partly a result of increased water content. Such foods are less nutritious and do not keep as well. There is a flavor loss as well.

7.   A broad genetic base is necessary for the development of new plant varieties, yet more and more old varieties are being lost as fewer are grown. These lost assets are irreplaceable.

Bountiful Gardens

For a select list of mail order gardening books, fertilizers and seeds, send a stamped, self-addressed envelope to Bountiful Gardens, 5798 Ridgewood Road, Willits, California 95490.
— A Project of Ecology Action

INDEX

FLOWERS

General 9, 18, 26, 39,
53, 70, 86, 98, 112, 119
Bulbs 18, 39, 53, 71, 98,
125
Wildflowers 20, 53, 77,
86, 130

FRUITS

Apples 15, 16, 35, 49,
95, 101, 131, 136
Apricots 15, 16, 36, 49,
95, 102, 136
Berries
Blackberry 9, 16, 36,
50, 69, 95, 102
Blueberry 16, 36, 50,
85, 95, 102
Boysenberry 16, 36,
50, 95, 102
Buffaloberry 36, 85
Chokecherry 37
Cranberry 85
Dewberry 37, 50
Elderberry 9, 16,
37, 50, 69, 85, 96,
102
Gooseberry 37, 50,
69, 96, 102
Huckleberry 37, 85
Mulberry 30, 50
Raspberry 18, 38, 50,
62, 69, 97, 102
Serviceberry 39
Strawberry 18, 39,
50, 59, 62, 69, 85, 97,
103, 119, 140
Wineberry 39
Cherries 15, 16, 37, 49,
95, 103, 136

Currants 9, 37, 50, 69,
96, 102
Dates 85
Figs 16, 50, 53, 69, 137
Grafted–mixed fruits
in one tree 52
Grapes 17, 37, 50, 69,
96, 103, 137
Guavas 30, 85
Jujubes 30, 85
Kiwis 30, 85, 137
Lemons 53, 96
Loquats 30
Nectarines 15, 37, 50,
96, 104, 139
Papayas 30, 85
Passion Fruits 85
Paw Paws 30, 37, 52
Peaches 15, 17, 38, 52,
97, 104, 139
Pears 17, 38, 52, 97, 105,
132, 139
Persimmons 17, 30, 38,
52, 140
Plums 17, 30, 38, 52, 97,
105, 133, 140
Plumcots 38, 140
Pomegranates 30, 69,
85, 140
Quinces 52, 140
Many other exotics 30

FORAGE, GRAINS AND/OR COVER CROPS

27, 59, 98

GARDEN AIDS

Books 79, 87
Fertilizers 54, 99, 125,
130

Pest Controls 22, 54,
59, 99, 112
Tools & Miscellaneous
22, 54, 59, 79, 99, 112,
141

NUT TREES

18, 39, 53, 85, 97, 107, 140

ORNAMENTALS

Cactus & Succulents
78, 112, 122
Ferns 21, 78, 112
Flowering grasses 79,
98, 112
Flowering vines 21, 39,
98, 107
Ground covers 21, 107
Houseplants 78, 135
Lawn seed 39, 79, 125
Scented geraniums
135
Trees, hedges & shrubs
10, 21, 39, 53, 79, 86,
107, 125, 133

USEFUL PLANTS

Aloe Vera 82
Broomcorn 9, 32, 85
Carob 30, 85
Chicle 30
Coffee 85
Cotton 85
Dye plants 85
Flax 85
Gourds 15, 35, 48, 68,
95, 112
Guayule 69
Honey Locust 85
Honey plants 133
Hops 48, 69, 85
Jojoba 9, 48, 69, 85
Kudzu 85, 95

Luffa 48, 85, 95
Olive 85
Pyrethrum 68
Safflower 69, 95
Sesame 69, 85
Sorghum 48
Spanish Broom 85
Tea 69, 85
Tobacco 35, 112, 119

VEGETABLES

Amaranth 48, 59, 80
Artichoke
  Globe 11, 31, 43, 63,
    80, 89
  Jerusalem 11, 31, 43,
    57, 63
Asparagus 23, 31, 43,
  63, 113
Beans
  Dried 3, 11, 31, 43, 55,
    63, 80, 89, 108, 126
  Lima 11, 31, 43, 55,
    63, 89, 127
  Snap 3, 11, 23, 31, 43,
    55, 63, 89, 108, 113,
    126
Beets 3, 12, 23, 31, 43,
  55, 63, 89, 108, 113
Broccoli—see Cabbage
  family
Burdock 56, 61, 80
Cabbage family 3, 5, 12,
  23, 32, 44, 56, 63, 80,
  90, 108, 109, 114
Cardoon 80
Carrots 5, 12, 23, 32, 44,
  56, 64, 80, 90, 108, 114
Cauliflower—see
  Cabbage family
Celeriac 23, 64, 80, 90,
  109
Celery 23, 64, 80, 114
Celtuce 12, 109, 114, 127
Citron 23
Corn 5, 23, 32, 44, 56,
  65, 80, 90
  Popcorn 32, 44, 56, 80

Cucumbers 5, 12, 23,
  32, 44, 56, 65, 80, 91,
  109, 114, 127
Eggplant 56, 65, 80, 91,
  115
Garlic 12, 32, 57, 65, 80,
  91
Ginger 44
Greens
  Chard 5, 12, 24, 29, 80
  Chicory 5, 12, 66, 80,
    114
  Chrysanthemum 57,
    128
  Comfrey 48, 65, 80
  Corn Salad 29, 65,
    80, 91, 109, 115
  Cress 61, 65, 80, 91,
    109, 115
  Dandelion 12, 65, 82,
    115
  Endive 12, 24, 29, 44,
    65, 80, 91, 115
  Escarole 57, 91, 109
  Kale—see Cabbage
    family
  Miners lettuce 80
  Mustard 57, 65, 80,
    91, 115, 128
  New Zealand Spinach
    5, 80
  Orach 80
  Parsley 12, 29, 57, 65,
    80, 91, 110, 115, 128
  Purslane 115
  Rocket 65, 80
  Sorrel 57, 61, 65, 80,
    91
  Spinach 5, 12, 24, 29,
    34, 80, 91, 111, 115
  Watercress 57, 65, 80,
    91, 109
Herbs 6, 29, 57, 61, 65,
  82, 91
Horseradish 12, 44, 91
Jicama 32, 45
Leeks 24, 82, 109, 115
Lettuce 7, 13, 24, 29, 32,
  45, 57, 83, 91, 109, 115

Mangels 24, 31, 45, 93
Melons 7, 13, 24, 33, 45,
  57, 66, 83, 93, 109, 116,
  128
Mushroom spawn 13,
  33, 67, 93, 116
Okra 13, 33, 45, 67, 93,
  110, 116
Onions 7, 13, 24, 33, 45,
  57, 67, 83, 93, 110, 116,
  128
Parsnips 24, 117
Peanuts 13, 45, 67, 83,
  93, 110
Peas 7, 13, 24, 29, 33, 45,
  57, 67, 83, 93, 110, 117,
  129
  Soup peas 7, 46, 58,
    83, 93
  Cow peas 67, 93, 129
Peppers 7, 13, 24, 29,
  34, 47, 58, 67, 83, 93,
  111, 117, 129
Potatoes 13, 24, 34, 47,
  68, 117
  Sweet potatoes &
    yams 13, 34, 47, 68,
    94, 129
Pumpkins—see Squash
Radishes 7, 13, 24, 34,
  47, 68, 84, 94, 111, 117
Rhubarb 34, 47, 84, 94
Rutabagas 7, 59, 119
Salsify 47, 58, 84, 117
Scorsonera 117
Shallots 34, 48, 117, 129
Squash 8, 14, 25, 35, 48,
  58, 68, 84, 94, 111, 117,
  130
Sunflowers 8, 85
Tomatoes 8, 15, 25, 29,
  35, 48, 58, 68, 84, 95,
  111, 118, 130
Turnips 8, 15, 35, 59, 84,
  95, 118
Watermelons—
  see Melons
Zucchini—see Squash

Notes

Audrey Ross, Silver City, New Mexico

Shawna Jeavons-Leler, Robin Leler, and John Jeavons
at the Common Ground Garden in Palo Alto, California

Mushrooms
(scale not shown)

May we introduce other Ten Speed books
you will find useful . . .

HOW TO GROW MORE VEGETABLES* than you ever thought possible on less land than you can imagine
By John Jeavons

" . . . the best plain-language explanation of Biodynamic/French Intensive gardening techniques we've yet seen." — *Mother Earth News*

This new edition has thoroughly updated the planting charts, information and plans needed to develop a garden rich and abundant in food, fruit and grains — enough to feed a family of four in the space of the average lawn. 8½ x 11 inches, 144 pages, $7.95 paper, $10.95 cloth

THE BACKYARD HOMESTEAD, MINI-FARM & GARDEN LOG BOOK
By John Jeavons, J. Morgodor Griffin & Robin Leler

This attractive handbook is intended as a hard-working tool for everyday use in developing greater self-sufficiency in a backyard homestead or in actually earning an income from a small farm. Covers tools, crop testing, calendars, graphs, charts, and plenty of space for record keeping. 8½ x 11 inches, 178 pages, $8.95 paper

THE VEGETABLE GARDEN
By MM. Vilmorin-Andrieux

First published in English in 1885, this book describes cultivation techniques that pre-date the days of chemical gardening.

" . . . a monumental work for the serious or inquisitive gardener, this book is a treasure." — *Co-Evolution Quarterly*
6 x 9 inches, 620 pages, illustrated with over 650 drawings, $11.95 paper

You will find them in your bookstore or library,
or you can order directly from us.
Please include $1.00 additional for each book's shipping & handling.

TEN SPEED PRESS
P.O. Box 7123, Berkeley, California 94707

Veitch's Autumn Giant Cauliflower (1/10 size)